MICHAEL PEARSON   RICHARD WARNER

ANDREW WARNER

BORROWDALE

Mikes-Eye

NOTES

Mike Pearson, one half of the "Mikes-Eye" partnership, moved to Keswick from York over 20 years ago and has produced audio-visual slide/tape programs for an even longer period of time. Several years employment at Whinlatter Visitor Centre gave the opportunity to use twin projection techniques and it is largely due to the encouraging response from audiences that in 1985 he joined forces with Richard Warner and started producing postcards and greetings cards of Lakeland scenes under the "Mikes-Eye" name.

In 1977 Richard Warner, then a design engineer, escaped the clamour of the home counties and, with the entire Warner 'clan', moved north to Keswick. For the first nine years the dream of living in the Lake District was sustained by Strathmore guest house and his photography now being called upon originates mainly from this era. When the time came to leave the guest house the family moved to Wythop and Richard teamed up with Mike to establish the "Mikes-Eye" business, recently moving into video filming and production.

At this same time, brother Andrew, keen to embrace the outdoor life, was taken on as a member of the National Trust 'High Level' footpath gang. After a few years heavy toiling in the fells a move to the Borrowdale Estates gang not only allowed him the chance to broaden his work skills but also brought him into close contact with valley life. In writing this book Andrew has blended his love of wild places and his experiences in the community to hopefully give an insight into some Aspects of a Lakeland Valley.

First published in 1995 by "Mikes-Eye", Riggs House,
Routenbeck, Wythop Mill, Cockermouth, Cumbria

Photographs © Mikes-Eye 1995

British Library classification
ISBN 0 9516220 1 3

Made and printed in Cumbria, Great Britain by
Frank Peters (Printers) Ltd.

BORROWDALE

Contents

INTRODUCTION

Spotlight on Derwentwater

Is there any part of Britain more beautiful than the Lake District? Certainly the north western Highlands of Scotland are wilder; Snowdonia more rugged; but can they match Lakeland's beauty? Is there anywhere that can squeeze so many diverse aspects into so small an amount of space?

Where to start? Ah the big fells, mountains in miniature, some stark and craggy, others round and smooth and some, most intriguingly, manage to be stark, craggy, round and smooth all in one. These high rough hills are at the hub of all things, dominating the valleys over which they hold such a profound influence. Economies, communications, social trends, they have all been directly affected by the eternal, inarticulate, inanimate fells.

Penetrating deep into the fells are the lush Lakeland valleys, each with their own particular and sometimes peculiar character. They are watered by crystal streams, and clothed by beautiful woodlands of

Opposite: Skiddaw from Calf Close Bay

7

Oak and Birch, Beech and Pine, a glorious paintbox of colour in the late autumn. And of course there are the famous lakes, the glittering jewels in nature's majestic Cumbrian crown.

There is more of course, so much more, always, around every turn, at the top of each and every hill is something new, fresh, alive, vibrant, just waiting, almost begging to be discovered by you – just as it has by all the people before you. And, if your heart rules your head, (and maybe even if it doesn't) you will be spellbound, just as the others before you. Then you will look again and you will discover new secrets, the secrets that lie hidden all about this magnificent land. Maybe the purple bell flower of the delicate Butterwort, perhaps the first flight of a fledgeling Peregrine, or the amazing colours of a quarried rock face in a working long abandoned. All this and much more awaits you, all that is needed are eyes that see and a heart that feels.

Maybe in that old quarry there will be a dawning realisation that there is something else that has left its mark on this very special landscape. It is the mark of Man. From pre-historic to ultra modern, mankind has left his fingerprints all over the fells and dales of Cumbria. From the fields in the valley bottom to the highest point of the highest fell, those fingerprints are everywhere. Who built that farm, that inn, that church? Who cleared the fields, who surrounded them by strong stone walls? Who coppiced and thinned that wood, allowing still more beautiful trees to grow? Who dug that mine deep into the heart of the fell? Who first walked the path that you are plodding up on your way to the first "top" of the day? And who built the cairn that you will gratefully collapse against when your peak is "bagged"?

Yes the influence of man is great in these hills, here he has brought life to a hard and barren land. Here is man the creator as opposed to man the destroyer, and his creations can be a tonic to a weary world, force fed on the pragmatism of modern market economies. In the Lake District, more so than in any other upland area in Britain, man has worked in harmony with his surroundings. It is this very special, and initially not very obvious, relationship that makes the region so outstandingly attractive.

The Lake District as a whole then is a remarkable, possibly unique, place. With its rich diversity of scenery and its idiosyncratic valleys it is a place that can never be appreciated at a mere glance. The thousands of day trippers that come in their cars and coaches will never truly know what they see, for the distinctive landscapes of Lakeland, clothed in beauty, saturated in nature, history and tradition need to be absorbed slowly. Indeed it is quite possible to spend a weeks

The influence of man: Robins Fold

8

holiday in just one valley and each and every day have something different to do, some new aspect to discover, fresh scenes to admire, familiar scenes to be seen in a fresh light and fresh perspective. And of all these valleys perhaps the one that gives most scope for this leisurely and detailed exploration is Borrowdale. If the Lake District is the most beautiful corner of England, then Borrowdale is the most beautiful corner of the most beautiful corner of England.

At the head of the valley, Great End, the abrupt termination of the supreme Scafell range, lies at the very heart of the great central massif of the Lake District. All around is a landscape that is so rough, so rugged, so magnificently wild, and yet it is still totally inspiring. Walk to the summit of Great End, stand on the rim of the awesome riven precipice, and behold Borrowdale! All is laid out before you, the narrow rifts of the infant ravines; the lush pastures and woods; the peaklets of distinction in mid valley; the glittering jewel of Derwentwater and beyond the beautiful symmetry of lofty Skiddaw; a land rich with secrets waiting to be discovered.

Borrowdale from Comb Door

THE LIE OF THE LAND

Dusk on Derwentwater, a thousand shades of pastel reflect in the still waters, the ducks are homing on the roost, while songbirds take one last chance to grub for insects. Evening is the best time to take the pleasant stroll from the boat landings at Keswick down to the famous headland of Friars Crag. Quietly and, hopefully, in solitude you can witness the tranquil last moments of the day, a magical transformation of colour from sharp brilliance through soft subtlety to shadowy silhouette.

Friars Crag offers one of the best views of this beautiful lake, a full length vista down past the wooded islands, Lords, Rampsholme and St Herberts, past the Scarf Stones where, in winter, Cormorants dry their wings, and on to the misty mountains at the head of the lake. It is a broad lake, broader than your average English Lake, and as well as its islands it has a shoreline clothed with magnificent woodlands, that is indented with many bays and promontories. In short it is a lake that is brim full of character.

Opposite: Derwentwater and Borrowdale

Much of the quality of the setting is influenced by the surrounding fells. Down its length the flanking fells are low, but display great individuality. On the eastern shore the fiercely precipitous Walla Crag and the even more vertical Falcon Crag provide a steep and exciting front to the much less exciting, indeed appallingly boggy, watershed ridge that links Bleaberry Fell in the north with Ullscarf in the south. In contrast, on the opposite shore, rises a smooth sided but impressively steep little fell with an enticing appearance. Its name is Catbells and it is one of the most loved and popular fells in the entire Lake District. It is the northern end of a ridge that leads south past Maiden Moor to the aptly named High Spy, a ridge that separates Borrowdale from the Newlands Valley. Not all the surrounding fells are small, for looming large in the background to the north is Skiddaw, at 3,010 ft the fourth highest summit in all England. From the wooded shores of Derwentwater it is seen at its best.

The heart of the valley

Despite being ringed by these rough hills, this sparkling Cumbrian Water does not appear to be hemmed in, indeed the feeling is one of space, of openness, of freedom. Only at the head of the lake is there any sense of constriction. Here the flanking fells close in, forming a barrier. From Friars Crag it looks as though the valley is abruptly terminated at the head of the lake, for, beyond this barrier, the big fells, Glaramara and the Scafell range, both prominent members of the central massif, loom large. Borrowdale however, is playing tricks. It is all a great illusion. Follow the main valley road, past the attractive double humped bridge at Grange, and you enter the great constriction itself. Here the fellsides rise so steeply that there is only just enough room for the road and river to wind their respective ways. This constriction is known dramatically, but quite accurately as the Jaws of Borrowdale. The road twists and turns, pulled and pushed by the very nature of the land itself. The tight arboreal confines limit vision; a hint of a craggy fell here; a magnificent tree, or a glide of emerald river there. Just glimpses. The Jaws are an enchanting place, but there is also a distinct sense of claustrophobia in their shadowy depths. It is then, with a feeling of sub-conscious relief as well as surprise that, quite suddenly, the valley opens out, light floods in, and you enter the inner sanctum of the middle valley. So secluded is this part of Borrowdale that each time the Jaws are passed through there is a sense of discovery, a feeling that never fully subsides no matter how many times the journey is made. The illusion is broken, the valley does not terminate at Grange after all, but Borrowdale now has new spells to cast, for it is here in this hidden and secluded bowl of green that the heart of the valley lies.

Rosthwaite lies at the very hub of the dale at a great meeting of valleys for here are the portals of the beautiful Stonethwaite valley which, although it has to play a subservient role to the main valley, is in fact just as big and almost as important. Beyond the village, over the shoulder of Brund Fell, lies the secluded Watendlath valley. This tiny hamlet occupies a fold in the fells, and is screened so effectively at its foot by low wooded hills that its very existence is a surprise. It is connected to the outside world by a narrow tortuous road from Derwentwater, and by an ancient path that crosses the fell to Rosthwaite. From this path there are tremendous views of the main valley which here is turned gracefully by the imposing bulk of Glaramara. The silver thread of river flows below the ancient oaks of Johnny Wood and is joined, not only by the waters of Stonethwaite Beck, but also by Combe Ghyll flowing from the remarkable hanging valley that has been scooped from the mass of mighty Glaramara.

At Seatoller, at the foot of Honister Pass, the valley turns south towards the big fells. The farm of Seathwaite marks the end of civilisation in the dale. Up to now the valley has been relatively flat. Now flatness ends and steepness begins. Here the riven streams of Grains Gill and Taylor Ghyll come tumbling down from the mountainous fells in foaming cataracts. It is in the heart of these big hills where lies the source of the River Derwent, the river of Borrowdale. It is the complexity of the middle and upper dale that makes Borrowdale so fascinating. All those valleys to explore, all those woods to wander through, all the hamlets that blend so well into the landscape, the rivers to follow and explore, pools to swim in, craggy outcrops to scramble on, and a wealth of fells to climb. In short it is a valley of satisfaction.

LAND OF FIRE – LAND OF ICE

Borrowdale: Land of Fire – Land of Ice. Perhaps a dramatic title for a National Geographic piece, but one that surely cannot apply to this lush, pastoral valley in the Lake District. Yet these are the two elements that have had the most dramatic influence on the shaping of the landscape, a landscape that has proved such an inspiration and a balm for so many people. It is the character of the underlying rock that is the foundation for so many aspects of Borrowdale, not only the obvious scenic features, the craggy fellsides, the unstable scree slopes, the massive boulders, the deep cut ravines and cascading waterfalls, but also the architecture, the husbandry, and indeed, in times past, the economy of the area.

There are in fact two completely different types of rock that structure the hills of Borrowdale, and both were laid down in contrasting circumstances. To see the very different effects they have on the landscape it is necessary to gain a little height to get a clearer perspective. An excellent viewpoint is the

Castle Head: Ex volcano!

15

small conical peak of Castle Head on the outskirts of Keswick. This can be climbed either from the Borrowdale road or from Springs Road, and a delightful sylvan path leads to the rocky summit. Look out across the lake to the fell of Catbells on the far shore. Its slopes are steep but smooth and grassy. Turn northwards towards the much bigger Skiddaw and there again the slopes are smooth, steep and slightly rounded. These fells are made from the same type of rock, Skiddaw Slate, named after the lofty peak that so dominates Keswick. Now look up the near shore of the lake. Here the fells are less shapely, their slopes are not just steep but precipitously so. There are big crags all the way along this flank and further up the valley are the knotted tops of Kings How, Castle Crag, and Shepherds Crag. It is plain that these fells are substantially different in character from their sleek neighbours to the north and west. The underlying rocks here and in the bigger peaks at the head of the valley, are volcanic in origin and known collectively as the

Big Crags & Knotted Tops:
Borrowdale volcanics

Borrowdale Volcanics. Which of the two types are the older? Well, the Skiddaw Slates date back to somewhere around 500 million years ago, whereas the Borrowdale Volcanics are mere striplings at just 460 million years old!!

The characteristics of the two rock types are completely different. Skiddaw Slate is a very brittle, fractious type of rock, breaking down very easily into thin shards. The builders and stone wallers of times past and present will assure you that it is useless to build with as it tends to fall to pieces when even mildly threatened with a hammer. Rock climbers also treat it with derision, not looking kindly on rocks that fall apart in their hands. Borrowdale Volcanics, on the other hand, are almost as hard as granite and consequently tend to break down into large blocks. They are very resistant to external forces (including brick hammers) and very durable. They make ideal building stones, highly adaptable, which in certain forms can also be split into beautiful, strong roofing slates, while in the form of rounded beck cobbles they can make a very good paving surface, as can be seen in many of the valley's farmyards. Climbers also love it as it tends, for the most part, to stay put when handled, a comforting characteristic. Fortunately most of Borrowdale is founded on these volcanic rocks.

What was the Lake District like all those years ago? Well 500 million years ago there was no Lake District, instead the area was submerged beneath an ocean. (A geosynclinal oceanic trough to be precise, but that's showing off.) As the shores of the sea eroded the resulting sediment was laid layer upon layer on the ocean bed. And so, with no fuss, no bother, and in a very relaxed manner, over a period of some 40 million years, the Skiddaw Slates were formed.

Meanwhile deep below the ocean bed something stirred.... the Tectonic Plates were on the move!! The huge crustal plates that underlly the Earth's surface were converging and the results were cataclysmic. Enormous friction produced a massive build up of heat and exerted enormous pressure on the surface rocks. In the end it all got a bit too much and... BOOM!!... the shores of the ancient ocean erupted with apocalyptic violence. The area that we now know as the Lake District became a hot bed of volcanic activity – a land of fire. There was nothing slow or relaxed about these eruptions. The resultant rock is comprised mainly of ashes and boulder conglomerates, there is relatively little of the more spectacular lava. It would seem then that the nature of the eruptions were violently explosive, plentiful, but relatively short lived. The effects were staggering. In the course of a few million years (just a blink in geological time) an estimated 20,000 feet layer of rock was deposited on the shores and bed of the ocean. And if that was not impressive enough the recently visited Castle Head is in fact the worn down cone of the actual spout of one of these very volcanoes.

So the rocks of Borrowdale had been laid, but there was still nothing that could be recognised as the valley of today, nor of the Lake District as a whole. 400 million years ago there was only a land mass partly covered, and an ocean partly filled, by volcanic rock. What would make this base structure into the much admired land of today?

Over the course of the next 300 million years the area underwent several periods of uplifting and subsequent submergence – those old Tectonic Plates were playing up again! During times of submergence more sedimentary rock was laid, whilst during the mountain building periods stress faults appeared in the bedded rocks, and the high ground was dramatically eroded by the elements, so much so that the deep lying Skiddaw Slates were eventually exposed. Thinking about it, this is what is happening today. We are in a post uplift period and the high ground is being eroded by the elements, albeit not very dramatically.

Finally, a mere 70 million years ago, there was one more massive period of convulsion, the Alpine mountain building movement. This time a huge dome was pushed up with a summit centered on what is now known as the central massif of the Lake District. This period produced a distinctive north – south faulting

Sleek and smooth: Skiddaw slates

system which, combined with the faulting of the previous orogenies, was to produce the distinctive valley systems of the Lake District. Funnily enough Borrowdale flows in a south/ north direction....

The Cumbrian massif had arrived. The fault that would become Borrowdale was already draining the northern side of the dome. What was now needed was the sculpting that would give the fells and valleys their distinctive shape. Slowly the temperature dropped, the snows that fell the previous winter did not melt, and gradually, as the temperature dropped further, ice started to build and build, and as the mass grew larger the ice spilled over and started to grind its way down the eroded fault lines. Ice, nature's Michaelangelo was about to do the business.

Glaciers, huge rivers of ice, filled all the natural weaknesses of the fault lines that were soon to become the major valleys of the Lake District. Descending under the huge pressure of their own massive weight, their destructive power was awesome. They took no prisoners, resistance was useless. And yet from all this anarchic destruction, something supremely beautiful was being created. Gouging and grinding, deeper and deeper, scouring the infant fellsides, the results were the fells of distinction and character, the crags and boulders, the rocky knolls and shivering scree, and the classic U shaped valleys that are seen today. And Borrowdale, of all the valleys, is a classic among classics.

Picture the scene, the great tongues of ice licking down Sty Head, Grains Gill and Langstrath, and all coming together in a massive joining of forces at a veritable Concordia Platz that would one day be known as Rosthwaite. Then, with all its combined power and strength it ground slowly down the valley, at first trussed by the resilient Borrowdale Volcanics until finally it broke through the restriction of the Jaws, and, finding the Skiddaw Slate of Catbells to be more compliant, spread itself lazily across the bowl that was to become Derwentwater.

Of course this is an average and very simplified picture, for glaciation is a very complex phenomenon with very few hard and fast rules to guide it. For instance at periods of maximum glaciation the whole Lake District would be covered – everything, even Scafell Pike itself, and yet at other, much warmer, times the glaciers would retreat, becoming thin trickles in the bottom of the huge trenches that they had previously dug for themselves. In addition to the main valleys, smaller tributary valleys were carved. Sometimes incipient glaciers forming on high ground dug out their own small valleys before joining the big glaciers which had already deepened the main valley. Consequently, when the glaciers finally departed, these small tributary valleys would be left "hanging" above the main one. Borrowdale has several of these, Gillercombe, Combe Gill and the Watendlath valley are good examples.

Eventually the overall climate started to warm and the glaciers finally went into terminal retreat. The last glaciation to affect the Lake District (and it was only a very small one) occurred just 9,000 years ago, which in geological time is a mere bat of the eyelids. What sort of landscape did these great icy sculptors leave? Well we can make a fascinating comparison with the Alps whose glaciers are at the present time in retreat. There seems to be several zones to each valley. The high lonely valley heads remain ice bound. At the foot of the retreating glaciers, in mid valley, conditions are almost desert like, bare rock, scree and detritus strewn all over the place, and with very little vegetation. Sometimes there are post glacial lakes held back by rock bars or moraines. The foot of the valley, de-glaciated for some considerable time, has a lush vegetation which has started to re-colonize the landscape. Val Roseg or Val Forno in the Bernina Alps are good examples.

Borrowdale was probably similar. There is evidence of post glacial lakes: between the Jaws and Rosthwaite; above Rosthwaite; and between Thorneythwaite and Seathwaite. These were gradually in-filled by alluvial deposition from the fells above and finally drained as the outlet streams cut through the impounding barriers. Even to this day Derwentwater is decreasing in size due to this same type of gradual in-fill. The natural drainage of the valley would not be very efficient but gradually vegetation began to colonize the dale. Conditions were not ideal and the resulting woodland was of dense, scrubby, stunted oak and birch. Boulders were liberally strewn everywhere. In short the valley bottom was a swampy, bouldery, tangled mess. It was in need of a jolly good tidy up. The scene was set for the advent of the last great major influence on the landscape of Borrowdale.

Opposite: A Borrowdale Glacier?

BORGORDALE – THE VALLEY OF THE FORT

Castle Crag

It was time for Mankind to lend a hand in Borrowdale, to transform it from a boggy mountainous wasteland to the beautiful inspirational vision that we see today. There is straightaway a question to be asked. Why, if mankind always inclines towards the easy option, did he bother with Borrowdale (or any other Lakeland valley for that matter) in the first place? All he was doing was inviting hard work. Why settle there? What was in it for him?

It has been generally felt that early Cumbrians settled the coastal plains and showed little enthusiasm for the mountainous interior. That is not to say however that they had no knowledge of the valleys and fells of the Lake District; indeed they had in some respects a very detailed knowledge of the area.

The stone axe "factory" in Great Langdale for example. How did they know that the Langdale rock would make good axes? As opposed, say, to rock from the Skiddaw area? And how did they first discover the

Opposite: The 'Thwaites' of the middle valley

21

exact site? Being high up in an incredibly steep scree gully it does not exactly say "This way to the stone axes"! And, if they lived on the coast, how did they get to the site? Was Borrowdale part of their through route? Could Derwentwater and Bass Lake have been an integral part of it? Although the evidence for this is very conjectural the existence of sites from later periods of pre-history does nothing to disprove the idea that the valley was being used by pre-historic man. Of the Cumbrian stone circles constructed during the Bronze Age the most impressive, certainly for its setting, has to be Castlerigg on a very strategic hill overlooking Keswick. Taking into account the size of the stones it would have needed a major construction effort. If there was hardly anyone living in the area why go to the trouble of building it?

The Iron Age also gives us another major site to consider, for Borrowdale had its very own hill fort, sited invincibly on the great fang of Castle Crag. Indeed it is this fort that gives Borrowdale its name – Borgers Dale, the valley of the fort. While not being on the same scale as say Maiden Castle in Dorset or the great fort on Ingleborough in the Dales, its strategic position is unsurpassed. Again the point to be made is that while there is no smoke without fire, neither are there Iron Age hill forts without people who need protection.

Did the Romans have any interest in Borrowdale? Well, their general policy when dealing with mountainous areas was one of encirclement and containment. This was certainly the case with most of the Lake District, although there is of course the spectacular road crossing the Wrynose and Hardknott passes that actually cuts through the central core of the fells. This however had a most important destination, the major port (in Roman times) of Ravenglass. The Romans never did anything without good reason. It is said that the Romans used Borrowdale slate in the construction of their major cavalry fort at Old Carlisle, but there seems to be very little reason for them to penetrate into the mountainous interior of Borrowdale. All the stranger then that there could possibly be a Roman road passing through Keswick, for it is known that roads ran from Papcastle and from Plumpton (Penrith) towards Keswick but the tantalising linking section remains undiscovered. Furthermore the Romans were sticklers for recording their achievements but there is no documentary evidence of a Roman A66T so, alas, until the mystery of the missing link is solved any theories as to the Roman interest in Borrowdale remains speculation.

After the disintegration of the Roman Empire it is possible that there was a reasonable population around the Keswick area, and this could have extended to very sporadic settlement around the lake and even into the Grange area. Certainly around 600 AD there were enough people in the Keswick area for St Kentigern to set up his cross at Crosthwaite for a spot of preaching. It is only guess work to attempt to understand their way of life but it is reasonable to assume that their subsistence levels were poor and that, as the saying goes, "life was 'ard". The further recesses of the valley would, if at all, only rarely be visited, indeed it is easy to picture the middle and upper valleys as being totally untouched by Man. This however was about to change.

As far as Cumbria is concerned the most important part of its history is the one we know least about. If the Dark Ages in general are a pretty murky era then this period of Lakeland history has all the clarity of a full fledged Helvellyn whiteout. What we do know is that the influence of the most fearsome of all the Scandinavian races was absolutely crucial to the social settlement of Cumbria.

The Vikings – the very name conjures up instant images. The great blonde Nordic warrior magnificently bestriding the bows of his mighty longship. The horned helmet, the Raven sails, the broad sword and the bloodied axe. Men of violence, plundering, pillaging, raping and ravishing; Men of Adventure, Men of Discovery. Unfortunately the instant image is a misrepresentation of the people who came to Cumbria and saw a land of appeal. There was no plundering, no pillaging. Indeed the Norse

conquest of Cumbria was a relatively bloodless affair, for the people who came to the West Cumbrian coast came to find somewhere to live, to put down roots, rather than sampling the instant but very temporary pleasures of the pillage.

The Vikings who settled in Cumbria did not actually come from Norway, rather they were second or even third generation descendants of the people who settled in Ireland and the Isle of Man. They were predominantly cattle farmers, and may have already been influenced by Christian teaching. They may have viewed Cumbria as merely the next place to settle, but there is a very interesting theory that they were in fact refugees, a sort of Viking Boat People. According to the Sagas, the people of the Scottish Islands together with the Manx Vikings actually had the audacity to bite the hand that bred them by raiding the coast of Norway! This prompted the Norwegian King, Harald Fairhair, to send an expedition to the western isles to put the upstarts in their place. The great fleet plundered the Hebrides but the news travelled quickly to Man and by the time Harald Fairhair reached the island the Manx Vikings had fled. If the people who settled Cumbria were indeed refugees it would help to explain why they pushed so deeply into the valleys.

Settlers; refugees; what does it matter? What matters is that these people were Vikings, and even though they came in peace, the Viking instinct was still there. There remained the spirit of adventure and discovery and of course deep down they were a mountain race, they felt at home in the hills, knew how to farm the harshest land. As they gradually integrated with the people in the settlements of the lower Derwent valley did the views of the north western fells send a tingle down their spines? Was it an inspiration? Did the Viking spirit of exploration take hold? Did they have to go, to see, to find out? And as they oared up Derwentwater towards the big fells, as they followed the sinuous twists and turns of the Derwent while pushing on through the Jaws, and as they finally emerged from the dark gorge into the sunshine of the middle valley, did they not feel the warm glow of homecoming, the sense of belonging, the satisfaction that the journey was over, the spirit of discovery finally sated?

Maybe it was not even like this. Who knows? What is beyond doubt is that these people were the first true Lake District dalesmen, the first people to feel at home, to feel really comfortable in their mountainous environment. And it is to these simple, yet determined people that we who are captivated by the beauty and spirit of Borrowdale owe so much gratitude, for it is they who laid the human foundations that are so crucial a part of the structure of Borrowdale. Slowly they started to clear out the tangled mess of the valley bottom, creating clearings where they could graze their animals, piling up the boulders that would later be used to construct the distinctive walls and building houses and shelters to protect themselves from the sometimes savage elements. In short they created the infrastructure for future generations of Borrowdale folk to build on.

They also handed down another fundamental and very distinctive element of the District, the curious Cumbrian dialect. Without the Norsemen there would be no fells, no tarns, no dales, no becks or gills. It was they who gave these very distinctive names to the landscapes of the District. Two other Norse words that are very relevant to Borrowdale in particular are tveit, meaning clearing, and saetr, meaning summer pasture. Think about it: Rosthwaite, Longthwaite, Stonethwaite, Seatoller, and Sea(tr)thwaite. All places named and settled by the Vikings.

Dramatic periods in British history seemed to have little effect on Borrowdale. The valley, mainly because of the surrounding rugged terrain, seems to have been insulated against any penetrating conquering forces. Only the Norse Irish settlers saw anything favourable in the landscape, and only then much later than in the rest of the North. When William the Conqueror invaded England, Borrowdale had only recently been settled and at that time, together with the rest of northern Cumbria, did not even belong to England but had been ceded to Scotland. Hence there is no mention of three parts of Cumbria in the Domesday Book of 1086, and it was not until 1092, when William II marched north and seized Carlisle that the Lake District came under Norman rule.

Following the precedent set by the Romans, the Normans adopted the policy of encirclement and containment, building several castles round the perimeter of the Lake District from where they could keep some semblance of law and order. The Norman monarchs had a policy of rewarding their loyal barons with gifts of land and Borrowdale was ceded to the de Rumelli's, Lords of Allerdale. In the late 12th century the Barony was inherited by Lady Alice II de Rumelli, a lady whose undoubted piety may well have been matched by a considerable business acumen, a combination that would have a far reaching effect on Borrowdale. Around 1190 she made her first religious endowment, the rebuilding of St Kentigerns church at Crosthwaite. Later in 1208 she sold the Manor of Borrowdale to Furness Abbey for the sum of £156 13s 4d. This meant that the whole valley, with the exception of the Manor of Derwentwater, came under the control of the monasteries, for the good Lady had also made a gift of the rest of the valley, together with some land in Keswick, to Fountains Abbey, the great Yorkshire Cistercian House. It was a move that would greatly benefit the people of Borrowdale, and it would certainly not be missed by the Lords of Allerdale, the poor quality of the land providing a minimum living for its tenants, and therefore minimal income to Allerdale. The question has to be asked: Was Borrowdale considered a waste of time & money?

The monasteries, unlike the more financially minded Barons, did not see the valley as a lost cause, and steadily introduced the methods of sheep farming that were to serve many generations of Borrowdale farmers. They encouraged hill farming, developed the existing settlements, drained the land to increase the pasturage of the "thwaites", and introduced monastic law and an efficient system of administration.

Grange-in-Borrowdale was the monastic hub of the valley for here the monks set up their home farm, (Fountain's was probably Monks Hall in Keswick) and it was here that taxes were paid and petty disputes settled. It could be said that the monasteries showed the hardy people of Borrowdale a new, more settled way of life, gave them a sense of purpose, while at the same time increasing the wealth of both monastic houses.

So, if the Middle Ages can be seen as a time of improvement in the social conditions of the Lakeland valleys, all of which benefitted from the benevolent patronage of the monasteries, it is small wonder that the Dissolution of the Monasteries has been referred to as "the Northern Tragedy". At first this was undoubtedly the case, for Cumbrians were amongst the leading lights in the anti-reformation insurgency of the Pilgrimage of Grace. The ownership of the land previously held by the monasteries reverted to the Crown, and was subsequently leased or sold to secular owners. The land in Borrowdale taken from Fountains Abbey, which included Watendlath and Stonethwaite, was sold to Richard Graham of Eske in Netherby, while the Furness Estates were retained by the Crown, a classic case of the absentee landlord and guaranteed to cause resentment. The monasteries had run a system where the owning House, although many miles away, was actually represented at the Home Farm within the valley. Disputes could be settled, grievances aired, and of course, the monks felt they had a pious duty to provide for the poor. Here there was a reasonable degree of give and take, but if you look at a social structure merely as a means of making money, you give nothing and take all, and inevitably the social structure deteriorates.

The new Tudor landlords, just as their Norman predecessors, found that owning large chunks of the Lake District was not necessarily a good way of making money. The land is poor quality, the turnover and returns small, and, because a living is so hard to make, the Lake District dalesmen always have been, and no doubt always will be, careful with their money! Against this background many of the new landowners decided to cut their losses and sold their land to the more wealthy of their tenants. And so came about the advent of the statesman class, the single farm owner, independent and accountable to no man. He and his successors have carefully farmed the Lake District valleys ever since, and it has only been in recent times that the social structure has once again changed. The history of most of the farms in Borrowdale dates back to this statesman era, and it was then that many of the existing dwellings were rebuilt in local stone and became such a distinctive and integral part of the valley scenery.

The 16th century can be said to be one of the key periods in the history of Borrowdale for not only was the valley changing socially, but the local fells were also being exploited for their mineral wealth. The discovery of the rich copper seams in the neighbouring Newlands valley and on the steep flank of Catbells above Derwentwater turned the area into a veritable Klondyke. Keswick became a mining town, German miners were imported for their specialist skills and an impressive smelting works built next to the River Greta at Brigham. Jobs were relatively plentiful, and the valley people prospered, for, as with all big industries, the mines required a network of smaller supply businesses to support them.

So rich were the lodes to the west of Derwentwater (Goldscope at the north end of Hindscarth was originally named Gottesgab or Gods Gift by the German miners) and at Roughten Gill in the Caldbeck fells, that the Keswick smelts were kept extremely busy. Unfortunately, smelting copper requires heat which in the 16th century was provided by charcoal. This charcoal, produced by slowly burning timber in a sealed chamber, was in turn provided by the surrounding woodlands and this very fact would dramatically change the face of Borrowdale for all time.

It was reckoned that one acre of woodland would smelt just two tons of ore and the trees of Borrowdale were quick to disappear under the axe. On the fells above the valley a combination of cold temperatures, poor soil and browsing by sheep and deer left the ancient woods with little chance of regeneration, a situation which has remained to this day. On the steepest fellsides, amid the crags and boulders, a few stunted specimens would have survived and, perhaps, from these came the woodlands which now tumble down the slopes in arboreal confusion. Only in the valley, protected from the worst of the weather and on the better soils, was there any chance of sustainable forestry. Coppicing, the act of cutting timber at ground level and allowing fresh shoots to grow from the stump, was the normal form of management. Production of charcoal would take place within

The woods of Borrowdale, used and abused for a thousand years

the woods themselves with the ovens set on pitsteads (level platforms set into the slope), relics of which are still visible today. Oak trees were the main source of raw material. These respond well to regular coppicing but unfortunately require a 15-20 year growing cycle and, inevitably, demand exceeded supply. Timber was extracted from all over what is now Cumbria and they even considered importing from Ireland but, perhaps due to the lack of timber as much as lack of ore, the industry went into decline. By the time of the Civil War it was all but finished, the final blow being dealt by the Roundheads when the smelts were 'ruinated and spoyled'. So ended Borrowdale's only major period of industrialisation. The

"Mountain behind mountain, rolled in confusion"

effect on the landscape had been devastating, but in the great unstoppable surge towards prosperity who needed scenery? Time and nature would gradually heal the scars, but it would take another 100 years before any value would be placed on the beauty of Borrowdale.

In 1769, Thomas Gray ventured into the jaws of Borrowdale "with that turbulent chaos of mountain behind mountain, rolled in confusion" . The first tourist had arrived and the valley would never be the same again. 20 years later and guide books were being produced. Suddenly it had become very fashionable to visit the Lake District, to cower in the presence of the "awful" mountains, to discover the "sublime", and to patronize the "primitive" dalesfolk. And the "primitive" dalesfolk have been taking vast quantities of the tourists' money ever since. Now, catering for visitors has become an industry in itself and very few are the people of Borrowdale who are not caught up in it in some way or another. It has directly affected the architecture of the valley, which now has many large hotels, built mainly during the 19th century. It has given many people an increased standard of living, indeed to such an extent that it is a very important and totally integral part of the economy of many of the valley farms. And of course it is a self multiplying industry and thus creates its own problems. The modern phrase for it is "visitor pressure". Can Borrowdale take the strain? Are the number of people now flocking into this and many other Lakeland valleys, destroying the very essence of what they are seeking? The great wheel continues to roll. Is Borrowdale at another turning point in its social development?

KESWICK ON DERWENTWATER

Keswick

Keswick is one of the great mountain towns of Britain. Its name is synonymous with the mountain scenery surrounding it and the setting is one of supreme beauty, lying at the confluence of many mountain valleys, an area known and revered as the Vale of Keswick. The position of the town is a very natural one near the junction of two beautiful rivers, the Derwent and the Greta. It also has many attractive hills surrounding it, Walla and Bleaberry, Latrigg, the Coledale Fells, Catbells, and towering supremely over all, the impressively lofty Skiddaw. Keswick has a close affinity to Skiddaw. Skiddaw is Keswick's fell and Keswick is Skiddaw's town. It is a relationship that is similar to Zermatt and the Matterhorn; well maybe not quite, but there is definitely that feeling that the two are interlinked.

The fell shows its finest features to the town nestling at its foot. From Bassenthwaite, on its northern side, it is a huge snarling monster of a fell; from Thornthwaite a great fat gigantic lump; but from Keswick

Opposite: The Vale of Keswick

29

it is a sleek, soaring, mountain peak full of grace and beauty. Much of its attraction lies in the symmetry of its form. The great central pyramid is supported by the bulwark ridges of Carl Side and Lonscale, while resting at the feet of the great parent are the two infant fells, Dodd and Latrigg. Everything is balanced out each against the other, forming an almost perfect picture of natural composition. In this great scene it is easy to comprehend the idea of Creation as opposed to Evolution and yet, whichever line of thought is favoured, the beautiful result remains the same. From this southern side it is easy to see the immense build up of the fell, something that gives a feeling of enormous power and strength; and yet there is also a feeling of benevolence, for the great bulk of the hill protects the town from the bitter north winds and the sun and clouds cast playful shadows across the great purple heathered flanks.

Skiddaw is easily climbed from Keswick by way of a path that is one of the most popular in the entire Lake District. Starting from near Fitz Park it goes firstly up the intriguingly named Spooney Green Lane. After an initial steady pull it flattens off as it contours around the side of Latrigg. On this section there are superb views of the Coledale Fells away across the far side of the valley. The path finally emerges at the head of the Gale Road and then continues easily past the beautifully inscribed monument to the shepherds of Lonscale Farm before commencing on the meat of the climb up the ploddy slopes of Jenkin Hill. This trudge is laborious and boring but as height is gradually gained so the views behind become more and more impressive. Finally, a short distance below the ridge, the path swings left, the gradients ease, and all that is left is a joyous romp, with the larks singing and the views breathtaking, all the way to the top.

What looks from below to be a sharp pointed peak turns out to be a ridge similar to the roof of a house, and, inevitably, the highest point is at the far, northern, end! From here at the summit the dominance of the fell in the North Lakeland scene can be best appreciated, for as the great panorama is observed it becomes obvious

Descent from Skiddaw

that all the surrounding peaks are lower. Even mighty fells in their own right such as the neighbouring Blencathra are subservient to the High Man. This is truly one of the few places in England where you really do, to grab a cliche, feel on top of the world. And if the cliche doesn't get you, the wind certainly will, for Skiddaw has the reputation of being one of the coldest tops in the Lakes. Even in summer it is raw, in winter it beggers description!

The return will lead back over the south top which is the peak forming the apex of the great pyramid seen from Keswick; it is one of the greatest viewpoints in the whole of England. Here laid out in a great panorama to the south are seemingly all the fells of the Lake District, the big ones, the small ones, all in their rightful place, all building towards the one great picture; and nestling in the midst of it all is Derwentwater and Keswick laid out like a plan on a map. The descent will probably be enjoyed even more than the ascent for now the hard work is over and that great view is always straight ahead commanding you to stop and look every few strides.

Standing by the steps of the Moot Hall in the middle of Keswick on any day in the summer season, amidst the milling throngs, amidst the pubs, the Hotels, the gift shops, and the expensive clothes shops, it is difficult to see any other function for the town than to provide creature comforts for the many thousands of visitors that pour in

The hustle and bustle of the town centre

during the summer, and, increasingly, the winter. Walk into one of these pubs midweek during the winter and the place will almost be yours. The odd local and that's about all. Walk into the same pub during "the season" and the place will be heaving; and that is one of the curiosities of a tourist town. A population of approximately 5,000 permanent residents swells during the summer to around 30,000 people and the servicing of all these extra bodies has become the town's major industry, its major source of income, and the source of the town's major problems.

With all the hubbub created by the tourist trade it is difficult to picture the roots of the town; namely the two small settlements of Kese-wic, the cheese farm of Fountains Abbey, and Crosthwaite, the clearing of the cross, which to this day remains the spiritual centre of the town. The granting of a market charter which was to have such a significant effect when the monasteries were dissolved; the great industrial days when Keswick became a mining Klondike; pencils, crafted from the black wad of Seathwaite, made in Keswick, Cumberland, a fond memory of school days; the writers, the painters, the poets; the coming of the railway, the going of the railway; all helped to develop the tourist town, but now all is forgotten in the rush to get to the nearest ice cream shop.

It was the coming of the railway that changed Keswick from a one street town into the rather sprawling place we see today. It was the Victorians that developed the intricate maze of streets between the Penrith and Ambleside roads, those terraces of stone built houses, many of which are quite charming, that now form the Bed and Breakfast hinterland of Keswick. It was during this expansion that a new parish was created with a new spired church, St Johns, built totally incongruously of pink Penrith Sandstone. The railway station, then as now, was a short way from the town so a big Hotel, the Keswick, was built right next to it and a covered walkway led from the station directly into the hotel. That railway was so important; now, with the closing of the line, Keswick's largest hotel is isolated in a back water and the railway station? A controversially funded, largely plastic, "leisure" pool. How times change.

It was the religious zeal of the Victorians that provided the inspiration for the world famous Keswick Convention which takes place annually during the middle two weeks of July. Christians from all over the world gather at Keswick for a fortnight of spiritual uplift. A huge marquee is erected in Skiddaw Street directly opposite the end of Helvellyn Street which is transformed into a Christian High Street of stallholders and booksellers. To many Christians the Convention is a great inspiration, and indeed many people on the verge of Christianity have taken the Faith after attending the Convention. For the local people, many of whom are not particularly religious, the Convention is a time of mixed blessings. Undoubtedly it brings more trade to the town, although the hostelries will probably disagree on this point, but the town does become very crowded, it is difficult to move around, and some of the Conventionists, those whose heads are working on a higher plane, can be a definite road hazard! Neither should it be assumed that everyone is at ease with the evangelical atmosphere that inevitably emanates when large numbers of Christians meet. Having said that if Keswick were to lose the Convention it would also lose a distinctive part of its character.

Keswick is a very cosmopolitan place, the Cumbrian accent is still just about pre-dominant, but only just. The town centre reflects this mixed social character by displaying a complete mish mash of building styles that have been all jumbled together as the town has developed. Built around the focal point of the almost church like Moot Hall, most of the buildings are Victorian, but there is also a lot of modern development from the crass short sightedness of the concrete sixties and seventies, to the more sympathetic and integrated styles of the latest pleasant developments around the Bus Station site. Indeed it was during

Crosthwaite Church

the sixties that the historic heart of the town, the ancient yards, the small alley like developments running off from the Main Street, were bulldozed flat to make way for two sprawling car parks. The chance to rid Keswick of at least some of its traffic problems by introducing perimeter parking was overlooked in favour of the need to get visitors to the shops as quickly as possible. Now not even these large car parks can cope with the flow of cars and there is talk of making at least one of them multi-storey, surely an abhorrence in a town such as Keswick. The sixties might have been swinging but the era had all the foresight of a myopic tortoise. Unfair..? Probably, but only to tortoises!

Keswick is, it has to be said, a great place to spend a holiday. Its setting is supreme, and this alone can act as a tonic to the most jaded soul. Its central position makes it an ideal centre from which to explore the entire Lake District; it takes all day to get from Ambleside to Ennerdale – having said that it takes almost as long to get from Keswick to the Duddon Valley! The town really does make an effort to welcome people, and in the last few years has seriously increased its facilities. The tourist industry does produce many facilities that would not normally be associated with a town the size of Keswick. Cockermouth, a nearby town of slightly larger size, cannot sport a cinema, or a theatre yet alone a W H Smiths or Woolworths. Keswick has all of these and it also has many features of beauty and interest. Great care is taken with the formal part of the Hope Park and the vibrant colours of the Rhododendrons in the Fitz Park, especially at Spring Bank, are a sight to gladden any heart. Indeed, the town takes exceptional care of all of its flower beds and hanging baskets which give a great show of colour throughout the summer. Next to Fitz Park is one of the countries more idiosyncratic museums. Here, within yet more Victoriana, amongst the more normal exhibits, are a set of Musical Stones, a sort of Flintstones xylophone, and yes they really do play, and, secreted in a wooden chest, a 400 year old mummified cat. It's a strange place, a very strange place indeed.

Crosthwaite Church, one of the most ancient and important sites in Keswick, is actually on the margin of the town rather apart from the mayhem of the centre. It does not hold itself aloof however and remains as approachable now as when St Kentigern first preached on the spot well over 1,000 years ago. Considering the significance of the place it seems a very unpretentious, almost humble building, totally in keeping with its surroundings and the people it serves. The church as seen dates from the 16th century, and was richly endowed by John Radcliffe, Earl of Derwentwater. It is a very dignified place and a feeling of calm and serenity falls softly about the gravestones. And all around are the eternal hills beautifully sculpted into the landscape. Unpretentious maybe but impressive nonetheless.

Crosthwaite as a place of worship is well over 1,000 years old but there is somewhere that is even older than this. Situated on a hill on the eastern outskirts of the town is the Castlerigg Stone Circle. As stone circles go this one in itself is not very impressive but here the situation is everything. All around are the high fells; southwards the Dodds rising up to the heights of Helvellyn; the gnarled miniature ridges of Naddle and Castlerigg; the sleek exciting outline of the Coledale Fells; Skiddaw is there as usual, but from here displays a strangely retiring nature; but most of all there is Blencathra whose bulk looms almost suppressively, dominating the scene. Look in all directions and it is easy to see why this small lowly hill should be chosen as the site for the circle. Really Castlerigg, not the town at its foot, is the focal point for the entire area.

Then there are the stones themselves, great chunks of volcanic rock forged in the depths of the Earth and bathed in the mystery of time; selected, transported and arranged – but for what purpose? A religious place? A prehistoric parliament? Who knows? What the place definitely has is an atmosphere that demands thoughtful contemplation. Unfortunately at the most enigmatic time of all, the Summer Solstice, the circle is used, and abused, by so called "New Age" people who seem to need an excuse to hold a party, a trend that is causing problems for the National Trust and also those who dwell in the vicinity. The place deserves greater respect. To catch the full atmosphere of the Circle it is best to walk there (walk mind!) at dawn on a crisp winter's morning and as the light fills the vast sky, let the imagination travel back through the eons of time, and then, possibly, there may be an understanding.

The fells give shelter to the town

NEWLANDS VALLEY

Hindscarth and Robinson

The high fells that ring the Newlands valley form an integral part of the wonderful backdrop to the Vale of Keswick, a natural link that has been emphasised throughout the history of the area. Newlands lies immediatly adjacent to Borrowdale, being separated from it by the Maiden Moor ridge, and sitting squarely in the mouth of the valley is the small but highly significant hill of Swinside. This intrusive little lump almost blocks the lower dale, and so, despite many visitors entering the valley from Portinscale, the natural approach is actually from the pretty, and geographically important, village of Braithwaite. Swinside and a lot of the surrounding farms belong to the Lingholm Estate owned by Lord Rochdale. Lingholm is one of a number of large houses built on the western shores of Derwentwater by rich Victorian industrialists; its gardens are well worth a visit when the Rhododendrons are in bloom!

Opposite: The Newlands Valley

Braithwaite lies at the foot of Coledale, a major tributary valley running straight as a die into the big hills that ring its head. The scenery here, especially in winter, has an almost Alpine feel to it, a combination of the soaring ridges of Grizedale Pike and the wall like faces of the aptly named Crag Hill. A good track follows the length of the valley terminating at Force crag mine, one of the longest worked mines in the Lake District, operations only ceasing in the late seventies.

From Braithwaite the main valley runs southwards, hemmed in to the west by the steep flanks of Barrow and Rowling End. There used to be a shallow tarn here in the lower valley near Uzzicar, and when this was drained the area became known as The New Lands, which in its turn was adopted by the whole valley. In this lower part all roads seem to lead to Stair, a tiny hamlet naturally set at the confluence of Stoneycroft Gill with the main Newlands Beck. In years gone by Stoneycroft was the scene of one of the earliest mining disasters in Cumbria, when the sudden flooding of the main shaft tragically wiped out an entire shift of workers. The valley mill, a relatively large one, and an important feature of the local community, was sited at Stair. The old mill is an "Adventure Centre" now, the mill workers tiny cottages, over priced holiday homes; a very modern sign of the times.

Beyond Stair the valley narrows and it is not until Little Town is reached that it opens out again. Little Town is both aptly and inaptly named; little it certainly is – a town it certainly is not! The hamlet has a superb elevated situation, allowing a comprehensive view of the complex upper valley. Here parallel ridges extend into the valley like the outstretched fingers of a hand, splitting it up into different subsidiary valleys, each with its own character. There is the great straight trench of the main valley; the secretive and totally secluded Little Dale; and the marshy wastelands of Keskadale which carries the continuation of the main valley road over Newlands Hause and down to Buttermere. In the midst of it all, at the hub of the valley, is the most exquisite church, a typical dales church, simple and strong in its architecture, and magnificent in its setting. Here the congregation really can lift their eyes unto the hills.

The underlying rocks of the valley are nearly all Skiddaw Slate – only Dale Head and High Spy at the head of the main valley have volcanic rock. This less resilient, more fractious rock gives the scenery here a smooth, sleek look. There are crags aplenty in this area but, apart from the ones at the head of the main valley, they are all broken and vegetated. The glaciers that once covered the valley found less resistance here, and, unlike Borrowdale, there are few examples of the spectacular effects of glaciation.

Little Town and Yewthwaite

That is not to say however that the valley does not have its own geological moments. In terms of fault patterns the valley is one of the most complex in the Lake District. Here there is the classic north/south faulting of the Alpine Movement as can be seen in the main valley, but there are also examples of earlier movements such as the east/west faults to be seen in Coledale, Stoneycroft, and Rigg Beck. This complex faulting, combined with the subsequent glaciation, has produced the high, well defined ridges that so characterise the fells of the region, and that make the fellwalking here such a joy.

Many of the steep fellsides are covered by a luxurious growth of heather, much of it wild and unmanaged, and this has made the region ecologically quite important. In addition, on the slopes above Keskadale and Birkrigg are two copses of old gnarled and stunted oaks. These are said to be descendants of the kind of woodland that covered so much of the District prior to the 16th century, and to the mass felling demanded by the Keswick smelts. It seems ironic that such a remnant can occur here in Newlands, in the very area where the Lake District mining boom started, and which caused so much destruction.

It is difficult to imagine that here, in what is now a pastoral haven of tranquillity, was once one of the busiest (never mind noisiest and grimiest) industries ever to be seen in the Lakes. Here as early as the 13th century rich deposits of copper were discovered and sporadically mined. These workings were later developed by the Company of Mines Royal in the mid 16th century. Some serious digging took place which was rewarded by some serious amounts of ore being won. The Keswick mining boom exploded into life!

These early mines were situated at the head of the main valley, and comprised of two major workings, Dale Head and Goldscope. The lesser of the two was Dale Head which was situated right at the head of the valley where two cuttings on the vein can still be seen, and which represent the St Thomas Works and the Long Works. The old

Gods Gift

spoil tips of Goldscope, on the other hand, are a very obvious landmark at the foot of the narrow Scope End ridge. This vein actually bisects the ridge and is easily detectable on the surface, taking the form of a narrow fissure, named as the Pan Holes on the O.S. map. It is worth knowing that the vein of copper that used to fill this innocuous looking fissure has been completely removed, and consequently there is nothing but air to fill the void! Here too the main entrance to the mine can be seen, but it must be remembered that old mines are dangerous places and that internal exploration is not encouraged.

The meaning of the very evocative name Goldscope is debateable; one explanation is obvious, for gold was indeed found here; however the German miners probably referred to it as Gottesgab – Gods Gift, which more pragmatically reflected the mines profitability. Copper was the glittering prize here, a mineral rich enough to attract the patronage of both royalty and nobility. Such was the wealth of the vein that it prompted a court case between the Earl of Northumberland and Elizabeth I as to the ownership of the mineral rights. Even for someone as powerful as Percy of Northumberland, taking on the monarchy was a dangerous thing to do – Percy lost, not only the mineral rights but also, following his part in a northern uprising, his head! Nobody messed with Elizabeth R! After the good Queens death the mines were worked by the Duke of Somerset, and continued to produce good ore right up to the demolition of the Keswick smelts by Cromwell.

Production continued after the closure of the smelts, but not on anywhere near the same scale. With the discovery of the very prolific copper veins at Coniston, the centre of the industry changed and the Newlands mines fell into intermittent working during the following 200 years. When they were taken up again the objective was not copper, but lead, a mineral that had been worked at places such as Barrow and Stoneycroft, but which had been deemed of little worth compared to copper. In the mid 19th century however it came into its own. New mines were opened at Brandelhow, Yewthwaite, and Thornthwaite, in addition to Barrow which took on a new lease of life, and dear old Goldscope where a very rich deposit of lead was found. First copper, then lead, all this mineral wealth certainly made Goldscope one of the most productive mines in Lakeland. For the next fifty years the Newlands valley was a hotbed of activity, the mines, in their heyday, creating employment for hundreds of people. Mining however depends so much on the marketable price of the ore, and gradually the mines became less profitable and towards the end of the century, one by one, they began to close. Although Force Crag at the head of Coledale kept going (mainly because it was mining zinc blende and barytes – not lead) Newlands mining to all intents and purposes ceased with the closure in 1921 of the Thornthwaite mine.

Nowadays the observant traveller may notice the odd cutting, and perhaps the more obvious spoil tips, but there is little else remaining to suggest such an ancient and productive industry. The big waterwheels that powered the pumps and the crushers have stopped turning, and all is now peace and quiet in this most intimate of valleys. Such contrast is absolute. It is as if the valley is trying to block out its blemished past. Newlands has had its dark satanic mills, and is now the epitome of Englands green and pleasant land. The valley bottom is lush, many of its meadows shimmer with buttercups, its streams are crystal clear, their banks wooded by beautiful survivors of the past. And, surrounding it all are fells of great character; the sentinel wall of Dale Head – as usual, perfectly named; the twin fells of Hindscarth and Robinson, slender intricate ridges supporting massive whaleback summits; the graceful ridge of Ard Crags; and the towering gnarled crest of Causey Pike. All are much visited and all much loved. The fells remain the same, but the scene they look down upon is transient, maybe not in the short life-span of humanity, but in the greater picture all is constant change.

Opposite: Robinson & High Snab

DERWENTWATER

Just as Keswick has its mountain, Skiddaw, so too does it have its lake, Derwentwater. Or rather is it a case of the lake having its very own town? Keswick's full title is "Keswick On Derwentwater", but the lake is not called "Derwentwater on Keswick", not even during the heaviest of floods. No matter, undoubtedly one of Keswick's great attractions is the beautiful lake, a fact that is indisputable given the evidence of the great hordes of summer visitors following Lake Road to its eponymous conclusion. No wonder then that during that great British rarity, the summer heatwave, the areas around the landing stages resemble the bathing beaches of the Continent. Here the broad green acres of Crow Park, Friars Crag, and Strandshag Bay, reveal the broad white acres of the sun starved British public. A veritable Costa del Keswick! This is no bad thing however, at least the scenery is beautiful and by concentrating large numbers of people in a relatively small area, other more sensitive spots remain peaceful.

Opposite: Derwentwater from Grange Crags

On the southern outskirts of Keswick is a small conical hill almost completely covered by superb woodland that is typical of the valley as a whole. This small plug of volcanic rock has the somewhat undistinguished title of Castle Head. Its size and its name bely its stature as one of the most important geological sites in the Lake District, not to mention one of the finest viewpoints. Climbing up through the cloak of broad-leaved trees, especially in the late autumn, is pleasant exercise indeed. A rocky step or two and the bare summit is gained and all is laid out before you, Derwentwater the elegant, Derwentwater the regal, Derwentwater the fair. It lies there, almost filling the bed of the valley, and yet it is not too long, nor too wide, rather it is just right, just the perfect shape and size to complement the surrounding scenery. It is not the outstanding feature of the area in the same way as say Windermere or Ullswater are, but rather it quietly takes its ready place in the scene, a picture of radiant, majestic beauty.

Just below the Jaws of Borrowdale the valley, reacting to the changes in the underlying bed rock, splays outwards gaining a greater width than at any previous point in its course. This greater width needs, almost demands, something to fill it, and of course nature has provided the perfect solution in the form of a most exquisite sheet of water. From the notched and ragged skyline of the brown fell tops, down past the jagged grey crags, and over the green canopy of the surrounding woods, the harshness of the scene gradually diminishes, an exquisite diminuendo that finally fades to the liquid softness of the lake. The extra dimension has introduced an extra element to the valley – water – and with the new addition the valley becomes complete.

Derwent Isle & Lords Island

The lake itself is probably quite familiar even to people who have never seen it, for it features frequently in television commercials and has been used for location work on numerous films. For people who are well acquainted with the environs of the lake this produces a fantasy acceptance problem. For example it is really difficult to accept Derwentwater as part of the Austrian Tyrol (Mahler) when you keep expecting someone to come round the corner saying "Now then lad, 'ows tha gaan on?" Even more difficult to accept is the idea of Borrowdale being the natural habitat of the Greater Spotted Hells Angel (Tommy). But the one that really took the biscuit was when the children in "Swallows and Amazons" went to sleep on an island on Windermere and woke up on St Herberts

Island, Derwentwater! Is that sleep walking or what??

That Derwentwater has been used so often as a film location is a compliment to its photogenic qualities. The surrounding fells with their mixture of crags and trees provide an ever interesting backdrop to the bays and promontories that form the lake shore. Friars Crag and the adjacent Strandshag Bay, so busy with humans in summer, in winter become wildfowl sanctuaries with visitors such as Goldeneye, Pochard, and Whooper Swans seeking the shelter provided by the lee of Lords Island. On the shore deer graze in the Ings wood, preferring to be as low down as possible during the cold months. Further round is Calf Close Bay with its magnificent stands of Scots Pine, and Kettlewell where the only lake shore car park on Derwentwater means that it is almost impossible to park for canoe trailers. Here the nearby fellside is very steep and craggy and it was in this area that Thomas Gray, one of the first tourists, noted with some trepidation that: "The place reminds me of those passes in the Alps, where the guides tell you to move with speed, and say nothing, less the agitation of the air should loosen the snows above, and bring down a mass that would overwhelm a caravan." Written in 1769 one might say that he was being a touch fanciful, but the crags above certainly have a reputation for looseness. A recent rock climb here was called "One in Six" after the number of holds that actually stayed in place when handled!

Autumn comes to Manesty

The head of the lake is gradually silting up where the two feeders, Watendlath Beck and the River Derwent enter. The shoreline here is marshy and after heavy rain the lake backs up, inundating the land, sometimes almost to the car park of the Lodore Hotel. At times such as these the attractive footpath across to the Manesty shore becomes an attractive paddle, shoes off and trousers rolled up.

All of Derwentwater is outstandingly beautiful but the Manesty shore is pure heaven. Great Bay, Myrtle Bay, Abbots Bay, and Brandelhow Bay, not just bays but delightfully hidden, secretive coves, set amidst woodland of Lothlorien splendour. It is a family place, a joy for young and old alike, and is easily accessible from the landing stage at Brandelhow. It is an idyllic spot for high summer picnics, for refreshing dips in the cool water, or for lazing in the sun. Summertime, and nowhere is the living easier than on the wooded headlands of Manesty. It is an arboreal Arcadia weaving spells of delight that soothe and refresh, that act as a balm and a tonic. It is a place for renewed discovery, no matter how many times it is visited, a quality only possessed by the very best.

The last of these bays, Brandelhow, is a great place for restoring ones faith in the ability of nature to heal mans scarring of the landscape, for here used to be one of the most industrialised sites in the District, the old Brandelhow Mine. Once there was a flourishing enterprise here, and once there was an ugly despoiled landscape bare and barren but for debris from the mine. Now we no longer have the flourishing enterprise but neither do we have the despoiled landscape. A good thing or a bad thing ......? And that one question raises all the issues that have to be resolved in the management of a natural landscape. Nowadays our society places value on areas of outstanding natural beauty, hence the creation of National Parks, but for these landscapes to have vitality and life, to stop them stultifying into mere museum pieces, the land has to be peopled, and for people to flourish there needs to be a certain amount of enterprise. It is the balancing of these needs that is the job of the National Park Planning Authority, but more of that later.

Many are the connections that Derwentwater had with mining. Very early on there was a smelt on Rampsholme Island (there would not be room for much else) and during the early period of the Company of Mines Royal, Derwent Island was used to house the specialist German miners imported to open up the Newlands mining field. This was the result of the antipathy shown to the miners by the townsfolk, not always has Keswick welcomed visitors with open arms! Once the mining field had been established and the Keswick smelts fired, the lake became the main route for transporting ore and other raw materials. It is a popular story that a barge loaded with Copper ore sank near the Lingholm shore, and thus we find Copperheap Bay on the map. Now the only transport that uses the lake are the pleasant launches which during the summer ferry passengers around, giving an interesting, if somewhat expensive, highlight to the holiday excursion.

The islands of Derwentwater, now all owned by the National Trust, have a very important landscape function, for they split up the vast sheet of water and at the same time provide interesting focal points. And, more important, like all islands they have a mystery, almost a mysticism that encourages the spirit of exploration. Apart from Derwent Isle all are uninhabited, but this was not always the case. Lord Pocklington

Mystic Isle

succeeded the German miners on Derwent Isle and built himself a sumptuous residence that looked out across the waters to his other home, Barrow House, now Derwentwater Youth Hostel. Pocklington was a great character arranging regattas on the lake and setting off cannons in order to be awestruck by the resounding echoes of the blast. The Picturesque Tourists loved him. St Herberts Island, perhaps the most attractive of them all, was named after the reclusive and pious hermit who made it his home. He was a contemporary of St Cuthbert, a man to whom he was much devoted, so much so that it is said they died at exactly the same time. Finally there is Lords Island the home during the 16th and 17th centuries of the Earls of Derwentwater. A devoutly catholic family they supported the 1715 uprising, an act which cost the third Earl his head. The night following his execution the Aurora Borealis, the Northern Lights, shone brightly, and were known for many years after as "Lord Darrentwatters Lights". Despite this damnable treason the estate was inherited, but the Radcliffes never learnt, and following their continued support of the Jacobite cause in the '45, their estates were forfeited.

Derwentwater cuts a great gulf in the complex of fells surrounding Keswick and by doing so has a dramatic effect on the local weather. The great ranks of clouds, surging in from the Atlantic and building one upon the other amongst the huge fells of the central massif, are rent asunder by this great rift. Large patches of blue often appear, the sun breaks through in huge spotlight shafts, the rain diminishes leaving the scene to be viewed anew as if the rain never happened. Storm and calm, the fresh washed renaissance of Spring, the shimmering haze of Summer, the cool mists and glorious tints of Autumn, and the grey steely stillness of Winter, the freshness of the dawn and the pastel tranquillity of dusk; all this great natural drama lies reflected in the mirror depths of Derwentwater.

The grey steel of winter

THE JAWS OF BORROWDALE

Into the Jaws

After passing the Lodore Hotel, near the foot of the renowned Lodore Cascade, the valley road switchbacks under one of the most popular climbing crags in the entire Lake District, known throughout the climbing fraternity simply as "Shepherds". The lake is now left behind and soon a side valley opens, giving an enticing glimpse of its sylvan charms. This attractive vale is Troutdale and many are the people who pass by its entrance without even realising that the valley exists. A narrow unmade track leads to a gate by some cottages, and as the gate is passed, and despite the fact that the mayhem of the busy road is only a few hundred yards away, it seems as if another world has been entered. Here is tranquillity and solitude, a shy, coy sort of beauty; like wandering into a secret. Ahead is a beautiful flat strath watered by a gentle stream that once fed the ancient ponds, still to be seen, that gave the valley its name. Beyond, the fell rears steeply and is clothed, as is so much of Borrowdale, in the most glorious woodland of Oak and Birch.

And there, soaring powerfully out of the trees, is the mighty Black Crag, perhaps the finest of all the Borrowdale crags. To watch the tiny ant like movements of climbers on its 300 ft vertical face helps to put all things into perspective! From the valley, paths climb steeply up through the woods to Black Crag and Grange Fell, or, less strenuously, over the shoulder of Grange Crags (which incidentally, despite its lack of height, is the very fell that hides the valley so effectively) back to the delights of Quayfoot and Grange in the main valley.

The approach to the tiny hamlet of Grange is very attractive, romantic even, for as the bend beneath Grange Crags is turned, a first sight is caught of the wonderful double humped bridge, that spans the river and draws like a magnet to the settlement beyond. The bridge has all the qualities of traditional Lakeland architecture in that it combines great strength and practicality with both grace and charm. In fact, so well does it fit the scene that it almost seems natural rather than man made, a tribute to the art of the local craftsmen. Just recently the character of the river hereabouts has changed quite dramatically. In order to prevent the river cutting away under the road, the bank has been reinforced by a wall of large boulders, which has altered the flow just enough to fill in the pool that formed below the bridge. This pool was used by Hugh Walpole as the setting for the "ducking", and consequent drowning, of old Mrs Wilson the supposed witch in the novel "Rogue Herries". In modern times what used to be a popular and exhilarating leap into at least 12 feet of water (summertime only of course – and then only during a heatwave!) has now become the equivalent of jumping off a diving board into a paddling pool.

The hamlet of Grange has an attractive cluster of houses around a rather scruffy green, but other than that has very few distinguishing merits. What it seems to lack, and what the other villages of the valley all possess, is a traditional working heart; a reason, other than tourism, for the village to exist, something to give it work and thereby life. Grange has lost its roots, is losing its heritage, is becoming a picture of what the Lake District would be like if it were to become a museum piece, a pretty picture no doubt, but one with no heart, no lifeblood. Of all the places in Borrowdale, bearing in mind that during the Middle Ages it was here that the monks of Furness established their "home" farm, Grange needs its sense of heritage. And yet perhaps this is wrong. With traditional industries being run down, and certainly hill farming seems at present to be going through a trough, perhaps Grange does represent the only viable future for the traditional Lakeland village. Perhaps in the 21st century what seems to be happening now in the Lakes will not be regarded as an ending, but more as a beginning.

A narrow lane leads southwards from Grange towards Hollows Farm (if only this was in the village!) and from it a track continues into one of the most beautiful areas in the entire Lake District, the renowned Jaws of Borrowdale. Here is a land of almost mystic enchantment, a land of trees and rocks and crystal streams, of groves and glades and craggy knolls, a land full of nooks and crannies just waiting to be explored. The track reaches the Derwent at one of its most beautiful reaches. Here an emerald glide reflects all the colours of the sylvan surroundings, before breaking over shallow cobble beds in a chattering ferment of glinting white and silver, the river widens and turns on its way down to Grange.

The path divides at this point, to the right a rough track climbs behind Castle Crag before continuing as a delightful terrace walk to Honister, while to the left a meandering path follows the river on its way through the Jaws to Rosthwaite. This lower path rounds a rocky bluff and enters a wonderland of low knolls, and beautiful mixed woodland interspersed with bright sunny clearings carpeted in soft green turf. The knolls incidentally were carved and planed by the mighty glaciers, testimony to the strength and resistance of the rock. They are known as "Roche Moutonees" – literally "Rock Sheep" – and, here's a fascinating fact, the toilets at Grange are actually built on one. Further on the path climbs a little and leads into

High Hows Wood where the ancient oaks form a perfect home for Red Squirrels (no Greys – not yet) and any number of species of birds from little Wrens to mighty Buzzards. Here the constriction of the Jaws is at its narrowest and the fell rises steeply. There is a network of old neglected paths that lead to old neglected stone quarries, once the livelihood of a large work force, now a resting place for penniless travellers. The caves here have the musty smell of faded history, not of glorious deeds on some foreign battlefield, but of sweat and toil and hard graft, of men trying to earn enough to raise their families and keep the wolf from the door. It is no more, can never be again – for modern economics dictate that to profitably quarry here, Castle Crag would have to go – times change and quarrying has little part to play in present day Borrowdale. Look at the amazing colour in the rock and be glad that it helped to build the wonderful houses in the valley, but do not feel sadness for the men who worked here, a pound to a penny says that any one of them would have preferred the "easy money" from a tea shop, a guest house or hotel!

On the far side of the river, despite the disturbance of the valley road, the scenery in detail is just as delightful. On a shelf of land some way above the road is one of the biggest boulders to be seen in all England, the renowned Bowderstone. Weighing some 1,970 tons it is the size of a "highly desirable detached residence of character". It is very big indeed, but what is most surprising is the position in which it has come to rest. It lies in what seems to be a highly precarious state, balanced on an undercut apex like the keel of a ship. This highly unlikely posture raises the question as to its origin, "Did it fall or was it pushed?" Was it once part of Bowder Crags, high on the fellside above? Or did it come from much further afield, swept along and deposited by one of the great glaciers of the Ice Age? Whatever the origin the situation is marvellous, wonderful specimens of Silver Birch crowning a multitude of rocky bluffs and boulders of every size scattered about. Near an upright stone there is a glorious view of the middle valley and nearby are a quaint cottage and outhouse dating back to the time when the Bowderstone was an unmissable part of the tourist round.

The emerald glide

From the Bowderstone a broad path leads northwards still amongst beautiful woodland, and passes below the steep outcrop of Wodens Face. Rounding a bluff it passes alongside the large and derelict Quayfoot Quarry. Until the late seventies the quarry was a remarkable place, the closehead (underground) workings producing a cave of immense proportions. During the fifties and sixties the cave was the social focal point for the local climbing scene. Now, whether their anarchical and rabelasian roistering got a little out of hand, or whether the quarry was truly structurally unsound remains a matter of debate, but for whatever reason the cave was blown to bits, resulting in the ugly and dangerous looking hole in the ground that is seen today. The old spoil tips of the quarry were the scene some time ago of a remarkable restoration operation. Here the National Trust brought in many tons of soil to cover the massive piles of naked stone.

The area was grass seeded and Silver Birch were allowed to colonize it naturally. Today it is a much needed car park, large enough to cover any demands, while remaining totally inconspicuous, a magnificent example of an eyesore being healed and put to good use. This act of restoration was very much in keeping with the traditions of the valley, man working in sympathy with his surroundings to produce something that is both practical and pleasing to the eye.

From the car park soft green paths radiate through an amazing hinterland of low hills, old quarries, and lovely stands of Birch, Oak and Hawthorn; indeed when the May blossom is in full bloom the trees here appear to be covered in fresh spring snow. All around the fell sides rise steeply, great crags spring from the mantle of trees their looming buttresses seeking the warmth of the sun. It is here in the Jaws, on crags such as Shepherds, Black Crag, Greatend and Quayfoot, Bowder Crags and Goat Crag that the individual identity of Borrowdale rock climbing is to be found. The source lies in the arboreal shroud that conceals the roots of the mighty crags. Here in a cocoon of sheltered security the climber prepares. The trees hide the difficulties that lie ahead, similarly they conceal the climber from the unwanted attentions of curious passers-by. The ambience is warm and friendly. The eyes search, the hands explore; a hold is found and another, an adjustment made, another hold and finally the sequence is discovered, the key turned and the climber dances upwards. Up, up, and out through the verdant canopy; suddenly there is warmth, light, a gentle breeze, space beneath the heels, and majestic beauty all around. And it is here at this moment of transition that the unique quality of Borrowdale rock climbing can be enjoyed to the full.

Meanwhile, back down on terra firma, that same beauty, sometimes bold and brash, sometimes subtle and seclusive, is all enveloping. It is a beauty that seems naturally strong, as strong as the trees, as strong as the very hills, but in truth it is a beauty that can easily be despoiled. In wandering through Borrowdale everything seems to be natural, unspoiled, unblemished; there are no blots on the landscape, no man-made scarring. All is as it should be. But that does not necessarily mean that it is normal, indeed it could be argued that this is very abnormal, for Borrowdale, along with the rest of the Lake District, is protected land.

Witness the great grids of power-lines marching straight line through the valleys of the Alps, see the grim gravel extractions that scar every glacial river. In Scotland notice how many of the natural lochs have been dammed and enlarged to suit the purposes of man; and caravan sites, see how many of the beautiful beaches of the west coast are blemished by the obtrusive siting of the inevitably attendant caravan site. This does not happen in Borrowdale nor the Lake District as a whole because development of the area is strictly controlled by the Lake District National Park Planning Board. It is this authority that is constantly trying to balance out the eternal equation. On the one hand it has the weighty duty of protecting the scenery of the Lake District while on the other, in order to keep the area alive, it has to allow a certain amount of enterprise. In practical terms this is administered by a planning authority that acts in the same manner as a local District or County Council but with special consideration for the protection of the Lake District environment. Bearing in mind what can happen without this protection, the Planning Board plays an extremely important, if somewhat taken for granted, part in the conservation of the Lake District and as such should have its praises quite rightly sung. Everybody who loves the Lake District should be thankful for the existence of the LDSPB.

In Borrowdale the Planning Board is fortunate in having, in general, the happy cooperation of the major landowners of the valley – the National Trust. The Trust was founded in 1895 by four like-minded souls; Hugh Grosvenor, Duke of Westminster; Octavia Hill; Robert Hunter; and Canon Hardwicke Rawnsley, the Rector of Crosthwaite Church Keswick. Rawnsley was an indominatable character who loomed large in the conservation and access battles of the late 19th century. It was controversies such as the 1882 proposal for a light railway to run the length of Borrowdale, from the Honister slate quarries to the main line at Braithwaite, and a big footpath closure problem on Latrigg in 1887 that honed the determination and vision that were vital to the formation of what is now a very far reaching organisation. The Trust is a charity formed to conserve the heritage of the nation. In the Lake District much of the heritage lies in the fells and valleys, lakes and woods that make up this enchanting and much loved landscape. Therefore the Trust has acquired large areas of Lakeland so that the scenic value can be protected and enjoyed by all. It is held in trust for the nation. In wandering through the wonderland of Borrowdale it is very reassuring to realise that this beautiful and bounteous landscape will never be unnaturally despoiled.

It is often said of people that the things that are most familiar are the things that are least noticed. Now a typical Lake District dalesman, or woman, is a person whose character matches the rugged terrain that is the background to their life. Tough, resilient, hard-bitten, practical and pragmatic, it would be easy to assume, especially amongst the farmers, that they are unsentimental and uncaring. Unsentimental maybe, but it is a false assumption to say uncaring. The valley people know their "patch" intimately (Borrowdale folk refer to areas of the valley by local names unknown, despite the guide books, to the general public) and are very aware of the slightest changes; trees being felled or planted, crags being "cleaned" by climbers, new motorway paths, guide book inspired, scarring the fellsides; – they see everything and, despite any outward appearance, have no doubt about it, they care.

For the most part the people of Borrowdale accept that the Lake District needs protecting and believe that the Planning Board does a good job. There is however a down side to all this in that the machinery of the Planning Board has become so large that it has spawned yet another faceless bureaucracy, yet more paperwork, yet more expenditure, yet another form of "Big Brother". In some respects the joy of living in a National Park is tempered by having, in small measure, to accept a restriction of the fundamental freedom to develop, inherent to all British people. Both the Planning Board and the National Trust have become very large institutions within the Lake District, indeed they both have a presence that very few visitors will have failed to notice. In recent times there have been worrying signs that due to their size these two very influential bodies have tended to become inward looking, coming up with well intended theoretical schemes, such as a ban on motor vehicles in Borrowdale, but failing to take into account the views of the people that the idea would most affect. If the Lake District is to maintain that special relationship between man and nature, the relationship that makes Lakeland unique, it is crucial that the protecting bodies work with the local population, gaining their respect, rather than walking roughshod over them, creating antipathy. In dealing with the problems created by modern day economies and social

The subtle beauty of the Jaws

tendencies, it is important that these bodies do not lose sight of the fundamental values that principled their foundation, the Lake District is far too precious to be allowed to fall victim to bureaucracy...... Fortunately there are no soap boxes in the Jaws of Borrowdale (although the Bowderstone would make a splendid one!) instead the message that is rammed home time and time again is of the beauty and splendour of it all.

The actual restriction of the Jaws is caused by the impending steepness of two minor peaks that have pretensions of greatness. On the eastern side lies the shapely cone of Kings How, part of the sprawling greater mass of Grange Fell. Approaching from Troutdale and clambering up through the steep woods – a real experience in late October – gives access to a strange heathery plateau; from there a delightful path through bracken and heather and over rocky bluffs leads to the neat summit and a stunning full length view of Borrowdale.

On the western side of the river lies the delightful Castle Crag, a fang of rock thrusting up from the Jaws. Steep, and almost entirely ringed by crags, there is just one breach in the defences. The best approach is from Grange via the old Rigg Head Quarry track which climbs a silent side valley and continues splendidly to eventually reach Seatoller or Honister. Turning aside for Castle Crag a path winds its way up to the foot of a great spoil heap of slate. A crazy track scales the nerve wracking tip and finally emerges on a promontory which gives wonderful views of Rosthwaite and the Stonethwaite valley. At this point a great quarry has been cut right into the very top of the fell and a thin path skirts this on the right to gain the summit. To think that this was once the site of the old Iron Age fort that gave the valley its name. Impregnable seems an understatement. Even the Romans would have thought twice about attacking this one.

Again the view is wonderful, Skiddaw looking particularly impressive from this direction, but here also Rosthwaite, sitting comfortably within its green fields, and Stonethwaite, with the truly beautiful Eagle Crag in the background, are also seen to great effect. To the south the eye is irresistibly drawn by the immense bulk of high fells from Glaramara to Scafell. It seems fitting that this small neat summit with its great sense of heritage should be chosen as a War Memorial to the men of Borrowdale.

There is only one safe way down, reversing the path of ascent down past the quarry. The stone so toilfully won from here will have built many a house in Keswick and the surrounding area, will have slated many a roof, built many a garden wall; but at what cost? Virtually all trace of the ancient fort has gone, a good third of the summit area blown to pieces, and that spoil tip, yes it's great fun, gives the climb a great sense of adventure, but let's face it, really it is a dreadful eyesore. That there was a need for quarrying in the 19th century, and, to a much lesser extent, even today is indisputable; but on the top of Castle Crag for goodness sake...? All around is scenery of the highest order, surely here on the summit of this exquisite fell it is possible to understand the need to protect this wonderful environment.

Opposite: The other side of
Castle Crag

THE MIDDLE VALLEY

Winter 'taks hod'.
Rosthwaite from Kings How

Bursting out of the close confines of the Jaws, into the wonderful inner sanctum of the middle valley is always an exciting moment. It is almost like entering a new world, a world of spaciousness, of freedom and of light. How neat and tidy it all seems and how refreshing it is to discover, time and time again, this apparently new landscape. It is a land of emerald green fields, of beautiful broad-leaved woods clinging desperately to the steep fellsides, a land of glittering streams, and fells that are gaining in stature and character.

The valley bottom here is wide, and extraordinarily flat, probably as a result of the post-glacial lakes that used to fill this section of the valley. The hay meadows and grazing fields are crazily interlinked, a jumble of green, but, despite the use of modern fencing, this confusing juxtaposition reflects the history of the agricultural development of the valley, from the Viking "thwaite" to the post "statesman" holdings

Opposite: Rosthwaite and
Eagle Crag

57

that are seen today. Here in the middle reaches of the valley the fells become more commanding, and pre-eminent in the scene has to be the mighty bulk of Glaramara, a major influence on the valley landscape. Indeed it can be argued that Glaramara (it means, rather romantically, "the sheiling by the chasm") is the main reason for the valley suddenly becoming so complex. The twin ridges of Rosthwaite Fell and Thorneythwaite Fell, encircling the beautiful hanging valley of Comb Gill, thrust forward into the dale forcing the Derwent to twist and turn, and, more important, directly influence the course of Stonethwaite Beck, a major tributary of the valley system.

All these glittering waters, Stonethwaite Beck, Comb Gill, the Derwent, and the lesser, but no less delightful, streams, Scaleclose Gill and Tongue Gill all seem to join in the middle valley to form an enchanting confluence, a meeting place. How natural then that here, at the geographical hub of the dale, is Rosthwaite, the major settlement of the valley. The village, regarded rather grandly as the "capital" of Borrowdale, sits naturally on the site of its own geological heritage. The houses are built around the rock barrier that once held back the waters of the lake that filled the entrance to the Stonethwaite valley at the end of the last glaciation. Indeed some of the houses have their very own natural rock gardens, and some of the villagers, by carefully excavating and re-soiling cracks in the rocks, have managed to grow azaleas, rhododendrons, and all sorts of other flowers in the most unlikely places.

In modern times the area around Rosthwaite has also become the social nucleus of the dale, in this respect succeeding Grange, its medieval predecessor. Here, in small space, there are several farms, the valleys only provisions store, the locals' local, and, most important of all, it has the village institute, the public hall that is the focal point of the social scene. A little further up the dale are the Church dating back to 1687 and the valley school which has such an important role to play in the future of the area, but which, like many other rural schools, has to justify its further existence to local authorities constrained by ridiculously tight budgets. The social interests of the valley are very traditional; informal sheep dog trials, hound trailing, and fell running are popular sporting pastimes, and indeed Borrowdale has produced both champion hounds and champion fell runners on a regular basis – it must be something to do with the water! In August the valley plays host to the annual Borrowdale Fell Race, and in September the local Shepherds Meet takes place in the fields adjoining the Institute. Both of these latter events have a popular social side and provide important dates in the Borrowdale calendar. All of this activity is so crucial in making the valley function, giving it character and life. What would Borrowdale be without its people? Take away the people and the valley becomes a wilderness, and Borrowdale, at least since the Dark Ages, has never been truly wild; rather it falls into line with the other mountainous areas in the world. The valleys of the Alps, the Andes, even the mighty Himalaya are all inhabited, the land worked, a living won; so too the Lake District, and perhaps here it is even more crucial due to the magnificent impact that man has made on the landscape. Just as mankind is an intrusion in the wilds of say Arizona, here in Lakeland he is an integral and some would say, vital part of the scenery.

Rosthwaite and Longthwaite from the Watendlath path

These middle reaches of Borrowdale are almost entirely ringed by the lovely woods that clothe the lower fellsides. Each has its own character. Castle Crag and Johnny Wood are places of enchantment, mysterious and intriguing; there is the tiny Scaleclose Coppice with its wispy waterfall; in the Stonethwaite valley the trees of Huddlestones Shop, a strange name if ever there was one, cling for dear life to the extremely steep fellside; finally Frith Wood, on the slopes of Grange Fell casts its own spells of sylvan magic. These woods together with the other broad-leaved woodlands that are spread so copiously throughout the dale and which help to make the valley so stunningly attractive, form one of the most important conservation areas in the whole of Northern Europe.

The woods of Borrowdale:
An essential part of the landscape

To most visitors the woods of Borrowdale are merely a charming part of the valley scenery, a glorious and extensive mixture of broad leaved deciduous trees. This is in fact only part of the story. What makes them biologically outstanding, so important to conserve, is not just the trees themselves, but the mosses and lichens that grow on their bark and on the boulders that are sprinkled over the woodland floor. The combination of a dense canopy providing shelter and shade, and a wildly varying rainfall gradient (the fells above Seathwaite get 130 inches per annum, which dramatically decreases with the fall of the valley so that Keswick gets a merely trifling 70 inches per annum) provides ideal growing conditions for this rather specialised group of plants. So rarely are these conditions found that collectively the valley woodlands are a grade one Site of Special Scientific Interest.

If any value is to be placed on these mosses, liverworts and lichens (the posh name is Bryophytes), and thankfully one of the redeeming features of this modern world is that seemingly worthless plants such as moss can actually have some value, then it is important that the growing conditions for these plants are maintained. Nature seems to take, at times quite distressingly, care of the rainfall, but the canopy cover is something that needs to be carefully managed.

Mans intervention in the development of these woodlands is nothing new, for their history shows that they have been worked and managed for centuries. From their post-glacial origins when they covered much of the valley bottom, through the initial summer "thwaites" of the Vikings, and further clearances during monastic times, the trees of the valley have provided timber for the people of Borrowdale. The history of the woodland reached a crisis point during the 16th century when the Newlands and Derwentwater fells were being intensively mined by the Company of Mines Royal. This era resulted in the massive denudation of much of the Borrowdale woodlands and it was from this period that the history of the management of the woodlands is evolved. As the mining activity intensified it soon became apparent that the woods, despite being much more extensive than they are today, were not going to be able to cope with the excessive demands for timber and charcoal that the mines and smelts exerted. The problems stem from the amount of time it takes for an oak tree to grow into useable timber. Even though the woodsmen

were carefully coppicing many of the trees, the demand still outweighed the supply. Consequently there is a letter dating from the mid 18th century that states that there were no "coalable" i.e. charcoal producing trees left in Borrowdale. Indeed much of the woodland that so copiously covered the valley floor and lower fells would be lost forever.

It would be wrong however to assume that with the closure of the Keswick smelts the remaining remnants of woodland would revert to being unused. What it did was take the pressure off, allowing the trees, by now in new stockproof enclosures, time to recover, either by their own natural regeneration or by judicious replanting by the local woodsmen. Charcoal would still be needed for other, more remote, smelts and with the advent of the industrial revolution there would be new demands from the textile industry which needed wooden bobbins for the new looms. The difference now was that woodland management had evolved to a level that could cope with this lower, yet still long term demand for timber.

This relatively intensive management continued to function right through to the end of the First World War, eventually dying out due to changes in the market, and possibly, from a lack of manpower resulting from the awful attrition of that conflict. It is therefore in the period, from the massive denudation of the 16th century through the careful management of the next three hundred years, that the Bryophyte species in the Borrowdale woodlands flourished.

Since becoming recognised as being biologically important the management of the woodlands has changed. The majority of the woods are now owned by the National Trust who work closely in their management plans with English Nature, the national nature conservation authority. The policy now applied is one of non-intervention, which means minimal working of the woods, no felling, no large scale coppicing, but allowing trees to naturally regenerate, so that as one dies, a younger one takes its place. It will be interesting to see in the next century the effect that this change of management policy has on the Bryophytes of Borrowdale.

This policy of non-intervention also includes non-encouragement of public access, not actually preventing it.....just not encouraging it. Therefore the nature trail in Johnny Wood has been closed and it is doubtful whether the existing path network will be expanded. Traditionally the people of Borrowdale have always enjoyed the freedom to wander the valleys woods, but nowadays this is not to be encouraged. It is one of the less appealing traits of the modern conservation authorities that their work appears to be shrouded in secrecy. How many people for instance even realise that the Borrowdale woods are a Site of Special Scientific Interest, yet alone the reason for their designation, or their importance not just nationally, but on a European scale? Are English Nature, by adopting a low profile, non-information attitude, implying that the general public are not to be trusted? Should the Borrowdale woodlands only be accessible to people with degrees in the appropriate science? With modern trends towards environmental and ecological awareness should there not be far more emphasis placed on informing and educating rather than disencouraging access altogether?

What is without doubt is that Borrowdale without its woodlands would be less appealing, they are a major factor in the landscape of the valley; but then again the valley is so complex that the same could be said of many different things.

Take a walk up onto Lingy Bank to the west of Rosthwaite for instance; here, looking out across the strath, the great portals of the Stonethwaite valley form a compelling picture. This massive tributary valley is a crucial part of the valley system, it is an important part of Borrowdale, and yet its scenery is so strong, so full of individual character, that it seems to be a separate entity, a place within a place.

Moon over Eagle Crag

The lower part of the valley around the very attractive hamlet has a classic "U" shape, the fellsides rising steeply from the green fields of the flat valley bottom, but it is further up the dale near the beautiful waters meet of Greenup Gill and Langstrath Beck that the true magic of the Stonethwaite valley is to be found. Here is an area of foaming cascades, of slabby waterslides and deep crystal pools, tree lined and set in a tranquillity of green. All around the fells display a raw ruggedness; crags and boulders abound; sparse, spindly Silver Birch cling to the slopes and ancient walls climb the steep hillsides. It is a clash of the elements, rock and water, that has created a wonderland of stimulating contrasts, and it is Lakeland at its very best.

At the very centre of all this is the attractive fell of Eagle Crag. As with so many of the most distinctive Lakeland fells what it lacks in height is amply compensated by its aspiration to grandeur. A mountain in miniature, Eagle Crag combines strength of character with grace of form. Its small neat summit is supported by big bulwark buttresses, the large, rambling Heron Crag, and the fiercesomely steep Eagle Crag from which the fell takes its name. The situation, rearing steeply above the confluence of the two feeder becks, acts as a cornerstone to the valley, giving it a commanding presence. The fell lends its character to the valley; what makes Stonethwaite so distinctive, so special, is Eagle Crag; the two are synonymous.

The two tributary valleys, Greenup Gill and Langstrath, each have their own distinctive character. Greenup is the lesser of the two, but stands in its own right as being a classic example of a "V" shaped valley, something quite rare in a region that has been so heavily glaciated. The valley is traversed by the old packhorse route over Greenup Edge to Grasmere, a route that has been adopted recently as part of the Coast to Coast Walk. In its lower reaches it has several pleasant cascades but in general is straight forward. Higher up however the valley turns and hides itself behind Eagle and Sergeant Crag, becoming shy and retiring. Here is an unexpected land of hummocky glacial moraine and big remote crags; Lining Crag in particular stands sentinel above the upper glen.

Langstrath is another matter altogether. Here the name says it all; the Lang Strath – the Long Valley. The name has a faintly Caledonian ring to it which suits the valley well, for it is very reminiscent of those long, wild, depopulated, and sometimes melancholy glens that so characterize the Highlands of Scotland. Classically "U" shaped almost throughout its entire five mile length, this is as "wilderness" as the Lake District gets. Tearing deeply into the great fells of the central massif, it carries the old packhorse route between Borrowdale and Langdale over the Stake Pass, and also a more modern path that follows the main valley to its source at the darkly forbidding Angle Tarn. It is a typical Lake District trait that more people will be encountered at Angle Tarn than ever there were lower down in the Langstrath. As these paths gradually (for the first three miles very gradually) climb the valley they pass by several lovely crystal pools, or dubs as they are known locally. Of these the most impressive, and the most popular for swimming, has to be Blackmoss Pot, a 20ft deep rift carved out of the naked rock. Lying beneath the towering buttresses of Sergeant Crag, it is an impressive place for a sunny day's picnic. Beyond Blackmoss however the valley shows its true rugged character and although to walk its full length is a wonderful experience, it certainly is no picnic.

The scenery surrounding Stonethwaite, as with much of the rest of Borrowdale, is owned and protected by the National Trust. In Borrowdale alone the Trust owns some 15,500 acres of land and as the major landowner within the Lake District has a large influence on the development of the Lakeland landscape. An organisation that places great value on the heritage of Britain, its most important function within this region is to preserve and enhance the essential character of the Lake District scenery and in doing so encourage that special relationship between man and nature that makes Lakeland unique.

The long valley:Langstrath

A large high-profile organisation such as the Trust will always lie open to criticism. This can range from the felling of a single tree, through to debates on national issues such as bloodsports or the nuclear industry, and it is these contentious issues that so often fuel the Press, both locally and nationally. While honest, constructive criticism is healthy, the less constructive sniping – especially at local level – sometimes seems to unjustly overshadow the amount of good (and often grindingly hard) work that is being put into the upkeep of the area. The record needs setting straight. Since money from the Lake District Appeal became available in 1989 the amount of work that has gone into Borrowdale alone has been immense: Over 3.5 kilometres of old hedgerows have been

renewed. The Borrowdale hedges are for the most part in a badly neglected state. The work involves repairing the earthbank, or kest, on which the hedge grows, fencing each side to prevent damage by stock, and finally planting the trees about eight to a metre which when grown provides good, traditional field boundaries, and, just as important in this day and age, excellent habitat for all sorts of wildlife.

There have been approximately 1.5 kilometres of stone walls repaired or built from scratch. These crucial elements of the Lakeland scenery take a lot of maintaining. In modern times there are greater pressures on the walls than in the past; on the fells sheep, and sadly, careless walkers have reduced sections to rubble, but really it is the roadside walls that take the most damage. The vibrations caused by the motor car are literally shaking them to pieces. Rebuilding them is like doing a three dimensional jigsaw puzzle, with as much of the work going into the preparation, as the actual rebuilding.

The fell footpaths of Borrowdale take an awful pounding and over eight kilometres have been recently repaired. A traditional technique known as pitching is adopted. It is extremely labour intensive especially in the gathering of materials. Once the new surface is laid, a lot of work goes into the repair of the horrendous scars, so that the ideal result is a barely noticeable path winding its way up an unspoiled fellside. The footpath work is done, not for the sake of walkers, but for the sake of the landscape, a fact that is recognised by few.

The Woodlands team have managed to successfully plant approximately 10,000 trees, nearly all of which are broad-leaves native to the region. Their work is largely geared to the preservation of the very important SSSI woodlands within the valley, and also includes a lot of boundary maintenance making the woods stockproof and thereby giving young trees, both new and naturally regenerated, a chance to become established. They also perform tree surgery work on individual specimens throughout the valley, and this includes traditional techniques such as "pollarding" which actually form an integral part of the landscape in places such as Watendlath. With more emphasis being placed on regeneration it is expected that less trees will need to be planted in future.

Over five kilometres of stockproof fencing has been renewed. This has been mainly undertaken on fence lines bounding roads or footpaths where the visual impact of neglected fence work is at its worst. Stockproof fencing, although not traditional is a modern fact of life.

Work has also gone on in the farm yards where a cobbled surface has been laid at three of the Trust properties. Again much work is spent on preparing the job, making sure cambers are correct, and collecting the correct stones from the beds of the local becks. Great care is taken in the laying of the stones so that the result is a strong practical surface that blends in well with the traditional vernacular buildings of the farm.

Of vital importance to the farmer are his sheep pens. Used almost daily these, first and foremost must be practical. Working in close conjunction with the farmers, four new sets of pens have been constructed recently. Built of posts and rails, these can be very complex structures; look over the wall (don't damage it mind!) at Watendlath car park for the ultimate example!

Big Borrowdale becks always mean big damage to anything that gets in their way, and two bridges have had to be rebuilt (building stone abutments actually in the becks can be somewhat irksome!) while two more have recently been resurfaced once again using cobbling techniques which seem to blend so well.

The Trust, like many other organisations, are becoming far more aware of the problems faced by the disabled, and to this end have spent time improving four paths, working on gradients and surfacing, to give wheelchair users a chance to get away from their cars and out into the quiet of the countryside. This gives many a first chance to see beautiful places such as Broomhill Point and even the Bowderstone.

All this work is done to a high standard in order to reflect the heritage of the valley; a lot of it passes unnoticed due to the careful use of local materials and the necessary skill to make the work blend. In Borrowdale the National Trust employs a full time ground force of 14 people with two part time staff. A similar level of work is undertaken on all the other Trust estates throughout the District and it is this unsung commitment at grass roots level that will hopefully ensure that Borrowdale, along with the rest of Lakeland, remains one of the most beautiful corners of England.

The National Trust, and the National Park for that matter, work hard to keep the valley true to its heritage, and now perhaps it can be seen that there is more to Borrowdale than first meets the eye. That is the beauty of the place, come back time and time again, there will always be something new to see. All that is obvious at a first glance reveals still more when the acquaintence becomes more intimate. There is, for example, right in the hub of the valley one of the quietest, most secluded places in the entire Lake District. Enfolded by the great ridges of Rosthwaite and Thorneythwaite Fells, Comb Gill is a huge upland valley carved out of the bulky mass of Glaramara. The cwm is a place of sanctuary, seemingly distant and aloof from the hub-bub of the main valley. This hollow is a classic example of a hanging valley and owes its origins, as so much of Borrowdale does, to the glaciation of the Ice Ages. Here a relatively small glacier was calmly and quietly carving its own niche in the naked rock, when, just as it was getting going, it was cut off in its prime by the main glacier coursing round the fell from Seathwaite, leaving behind this amazing amphitheatre of nature.

Two tracks give access to the cwm, one on the eastern side leading to an old corn mill that dates back in part to 1546 and has machinery dating from the 1760s. Here the old wheel can still be seen as can the course of the feeder leat parallel to the beck. The other track enters the cwm on the western side and has become very popular as an approach to Glaramara. Climbing steadily up through charming fields sparsely wooded by silver birch, the fell gate is gained and splashing cascades are to be seen in the beck below. A little further on a small cairn is reached and here, staying low, a small path goes left into the cwm. Soon the crowds plodding up the ribbon of stones onto Thorneythwaite Fell are out of sight and out of mind allowing the quiet splendour of the corrie to settle softly on the soul.

The further into the cwm, the more impressive the scene. Here is an amazing amphitheatre almost completely encircled by great crags, some large and rambling, others slender and soaring, some dark and brooding and some that are sunny and bright. There are few better places to climb. The bottom of the corrie is a strange sight; hummocky moraines, deposited by the departing glacier, rising haphazardly from their marshy surrounds. All this natural scenery is good, very very good, but here there is something even more impressive than the quality of the landscape. Here, within the depths of the fell, is a still, breathless silence. There is a much used image of "crags as Cathedrals of Stone" which, in many respects, is overdone as the constructions of Man very rarely match the awesome soaring splendour of the great natural buttresses of rock, but here in Comb Gill the silence, not the scenery, has an aura of reverence, something more commonly felt in the great cathedrals of the world.

Opposite: Comb Gill

WATENDLATH

Ashness Bridge

Only comprising three small farmhouses, the tiny hamlet of Watendlath holds a status in the affections of Lakeland devotees out of all proportion to its size. Much of this popularity can be attributed to the hamlets unique situation, occupying a deep trench which was carved from the hilly mass between Thirlmere and Borrowdale by a strong subsidiary glacier (which in turn could have been an overspill of the large Stonethwaite glacier) towards the end of the Ice Age. Gouging and grinding its way down the Watendlath fault line, it was cut off by the main Borrowdale glacier near Lodore, leaving in its wake a classical "U" shaped hanging valley hidden secretly between the fells. This total seclusion and inaccessability gives the valley a special atmosphere, a sense of independence, but this is an illusion for the Watendlath valley is in fact a reflection in miniature of Borrowdale as a whole.

Opposite: The Watendlath Valley

The valley has several approaches, none of them easy. First there is the narrow and tortuous road which gives vehicular access to the hamlet. It is an interesting strip of tarmac, passing through a series of unlikely situations, before terminating in a very definite full stop at the hamlet. On no account a road for the nervous or inexperienced, the conflicting shenanagens of the traffic does provide an amusing diversion for those making their leisurely, not to mention less stressful, way on foot. Leaving the main valley at Ashness Gate, the road climbs steadily until it reaches a small and innocuous looking bridge. Only when this is viewed from further up the beck does the significance become apparent, for this is the famous Ashness Bridge, perhaps the most photographed vista in the Lake District. The curved arch of the sturdy little bridge forms an interesting foreground to a glorious scene that is typically Lakeland, a muddled mixture of trees and crags and water and fells. When a light mist fills the valley, and the leaves of the Silver Birch have turned a delicate yellow, when the first snows of the year have dusted the top of Skiddaw, then Ashness Bridge transcends its hackneyed image to become a vision of almost unbelievable splendour.

A primeval mist wreathes Lodore

Further on, the road, which has only been tarmaced within living memory, passes through the beautiful Ashness Woods, another wonderful mixture of Oak and Birch, but also containing some Larch. As the temperatures start to drop at the onset of winter, it is possible, early in the morning, to see Red Deer sheltering in the woods. Escapees from the North West Water Authorities herd that graze the Armboth Fells, these seem to have taken a liking to Borrowdale, and a fair size herd now occupies the valley. The woodlands have developed in a strange hinterland area at the rear of the steep facade of crags that border the main valley in the region of Lodore. For one and a half tortuous miles the road has in fact climbed steadily across the steep flanks of Ashness Fell. Emerging suddenly from the trees, it finally gains entry to the secluded Watendlath valley.

A more natural approach to the valley is to start at Lodore near the celebrated Falls. These splendid cascades mark the final plunge of Watendlath Beck down to the main valley and ultimately Derwentwater. Only after heavy rain will they be:

> " ... rattling and battling
> And shaking and quaking
> And pouring and roaring....."

Most of the time:

> The stream is so fickle
> As to be but a trickle

> With apologies to Robert Southey

A good start can be made from High Lodore Farm by ascending Ladder Brow. No hope of a road here, instead a steep but pleasant path climbs to the broad col between Brown Dodd and Shepherds Crag. A slight descent and the beck is reached at another "toiling and boiling" waterfall, a smaller version of the main falls now further downstream.

The path then climbs again, but easier now, through Ashness Woods, an amble made fascinating by the myriad wood ants nests to be found in this area. Look carefully...... those piles of wood chippings are alive!! Finally, passing between the large knolls of Mossmire Coppice, the path emerges into the shy and retiring hanging valley.

And so, by whichever route, a new, somehow private land is about to be discovered. Ahead, for the next mile, the valley runs as straight as a die. The narrow, green strath of the valley bottom is hemmed in by the steep craggy fellsides of Reecastle and Caffel Side. It is an intimate landscape, the home of the Buzzard and the Peregrine; the delightful beck chatters along happily, Trout swim in the pools and Dippers bob in and out of the water in their difficult quest for food. At the far end of this remarkably level strath – after torrential rain it has been known for this part of the valley to become a lake – the dale is blocked by a rock bar, over which the beck crashes in a foaming maelstrom, the so called Devils Punch Bowl, an awesome sight when in spate.

A fold in the fells: Watendlath valley from Goats Crag

On cresting this final rise, and remaining hidden to the very last, there lie the buildings of Watendlath. Here is civilisation in the middle of nowhere, a tiny enclave of humanity surrounded by the wilds of nature. Here the valley opens out into a wide bowl, partly filled by a beautiful tarn. It lies open to the four winds, but also open to any available sunshine, something which must make hamlets such as Stonethwaite, which in winter exist in permanent shadow, more than a trifle envious. The head of the valley is blocked off, not by peaks with the quality of a Great End or a Gable, but rather by a wild tangle of heathery fells, not immediately endearing, but which require an unhurried exploration in order to feel their true quality.

Perfectly set on the shores of the elliptical tarn, a mirror mere reflecting all the colours and moods of Earth and Sky, the hamlet has been very aptly named by the Norsemen who first came this way; Watendlath – the barn at the end of the lake. Quietly attractive, much of the charm of the place lies in the mixture of architectural forms, and the curious, almost haphazard, relationship the various groups of buildings have to each other; here a group of barns, there an old farmhouse, downstream the sturdy little packhorse bridge, all mixed together, and occupying, in the lee of the rock bar and on the shores of the tarn, one of the most beautiful and natural settings in Borrowdale.

Originally a purely farming hamlet, Watendlath in days gone by, was considerably bigger and more populated than it is now. According to early maps, there were extra buildings near the tarn and also some in what is now the car park. It is said that at one time the hamlet had an Inn and a woollen mill, but all these buildings are now gone, and what is now seen is a streamlined and rationalized Watendlath, providing a living for its people, but nothing more. The history of this hamlet provides a reflection of the development of hill farms throughout the Lake District, a history that is engrained in the land.

Watendlath was first used by the Norsemen as a saeter, a summer pasture, and it was not until the lands were acquired by the monks of Fountains Abbey who introduced more intensive farming techniques, that the hamlet became permanently settled. It was also during this era that the extensive network of bridleways evolved, linking together the scattered hamlets and farms. Thus, from Watendlath, a somewhat soggy track leads southeast via Harrop Tarn to Wythburn, while to the west, the old packhorse route coming up over the shoulder of Brund Fell from Rosthwaite, gives perhaps the finest approach to this secluded valley. With the dissolution of the Monasteries came a breaking down of the great estates into smaller privately owned lots, the "statesman" era.

The upkeep of the land had now fallen to individual farmers who applied and developed the hill farming techniques inherent from their past. The work was very labour intensive, additional hands were hired at the annual hiring fairs; boundaries had to be maintained, walls built and repaired, hedges cut and laid; the intake fields, so essential during the winter, and also for the crucial hay crop, had to be carefully maintained, gutters had to be cleaned and drains kept clear. Some fields had a limited amount of crops grown on them, coarse cereals and "taties", and they kept more cattle which in turn during the winter needed both feed and bedding. In the old days horses were a crucial part of the farm, providing transport and also pulling power for ploughs and cutters; they were the "tractors" of the past, and like the tractors of today, needed their own special maintenance. It was all hard work, which doesn't, from this cosy distance, need to be romanticised, but for the most part, due to the number of people involved, the standards of husbandry were high, and the quality of the landscape was consequently improved.

Life on a hill farm has always been lived close to the edge. So many factors are outside the control of the farmer and the worst of these is definitely market prices. If the price of livestock goes down it is the farmer who suffers, and hill farming has never been an easy way of making a fortune. It is the market more than anything that has pushed the hill farm into decline. So much of the scenic heritage of this country has been in the guardianship of these solid pragmatic men and women, who put so much in, to get so little out. But if it is so hard and so unrewarding why do people do it? Not for the steady income that is for sure, but farming seems to be a way of life, something that is in peoples blood; it is something they just have to do; but it is not necessarily inherent, and it is easy to understand why so many people, especially the younger ones, turn away from farming in order to find easier and more secure employment. Ever since the Industrial Revolution, the city has always tempted.

The ancient packhorse approach to the hamlet

Because of this insecurity, the inheritance of the farm has never been certain. If the retiring farmer has nobody to pass it on to, then the farm is put up for sale. In the old days this was quite straightforward, the farm buildings, land, and animals being sold as an entity and as a going concern. The situation these days is different; with housing markets being inflated (in the Lake District, as in so many other scenic areas this has been artificially raised by "second home" owners) the farm as a whole is seldom seen as viable and so the Farmhouse, out buildings, and land are sold in separate lots. As often as not the house is bought at a ridiculous price by a non farming person, the land gets split up and sold reasonably cheaply and the net outcome is that the farm as such ceases to exist leaving more land to be worked by fewer people, and inevitably the landscape suffers. When this landscape is important either for scenic, or

Hay stooks: A thing of the past

ecological reasons (or, as in so much of Borrowdale, for both reasons) then it has become the policy of the National Trust to step in and buy the farm, subsequently letting it to enthusiastic tenants who, in conjunction with the Trusts estate staff, can work the land and keep it, as much as possible, in good repair. This policy has ironically brought the wheel full circle and now, out of eleven working farms in Borrowdale, only one is independent, the rest belonging to either the Trust or Lodore Estates.

Over the last fifty years the farming communities have become more depopulated than ever. Even at Watendlath, the acreage that until recently was worked by nine men is now worked by just two. Market prices, less demand for too much lamb, increased imports, over production, have all made the hill farm less viable. If the farm is not paying the first thing to do is cut overheads, and the greatest of these is extra wages. Hired hands, once essential to the upkeep of a farm, are now kept to a minimum. Mechanisation; tractors, quad bikes et al., have helped to increase the efficiency of the farm; one man can now do the work of several. The modern trend of cutting silage (which is much more practical in such a wet climate) rather than making hay, is one of the upshots of mechanisation, and employs far fewer people. Priorities too have changed; if the land provides a living for fewer people, then essential jobs take priority over less essential ones, it is far quicker to wire up a wall gap, than to rebuild it. And there is the rub, modern market economies dictate that a farm can only provide a livelihood for a very limited number of people, fewer people means non-essential jobs remain undone, and the thing that suffers most is the quality of the landscape.

It is now doubtful that any hill farm would actually be viable without direct aid from government in the form of subsidies. Ironically the amount of subsidy is calculated per head of sheep; the more sheep, the more subsidy, the less demand at market. The amount of subsidies paid, not only to Cumbrian hill farmers but throughout the European Community, has been a major source of controversy during the GATT negotiations, and it will be interesting to see the effect this world agreement has on the market.

Subsidies have their good points in that they help maintain a way of life that is important to the well being of the countryside, but there is also a knock-on effect in that, with the emphasis being placed on the size of the flock, a lot of the land has been over-grazed, a case of too many sheep on too few acres. This becomes a problem where rarer habitat types such as heath become affected and it is not unknown for English Nature to step in with compensation paid to the farmer in return for a reduction of the flock. This more conservational approach has been taken a stage further with the setting up of the "E.S.A." system, whereby money is granted to farmers living in designated "Environmentally Sensitive Areas" . With this scheme the farmers receive a compensatory payment in return for regulating the size of their flock, and taking a more organic approach to the fertilisation of their intake land. Further payments can be received for landscape work such as rebuilding walls, replacing hedgerows, returning to organically fertilized flower rich meadows and many more such things. In this way it is hoped to move the emphasis away from the mass production of unwanted sheep, and back to the restoration of the landscape. In addition to this, modern farmers have to be far more aware of the environment in the methods they employ, with bodies such as the National Rivers Authority no longer willing to turn a blind eye to the less "green" activities of the farm. A more conservational approach may be better overall, but it can be a costly affair in the short term.

At the present time the hill farmer is still in somewhat of a quandary; subsidies are going to be cut with a consequential loss of income. If the farmer is in an "E.S.A." (and most of the Lake District has been designated), he can still claim Government help; but if he does so, he has to regulate the size of his flock. This is fine, unless the Government decide the system is not working properly; a quick change of policy could leave many a farmer, committed to "E.S.A.", up to his armpits "in t' midden". And what about the poor soul not covered by "E.S.A."? The edge is getting that bit nearer.

No wonder then that, against this background of uncertainty, the modern hill farmer makes his money where he can. Nearly all the working farms in Borrowdale supplement their income with some Bed and Breakfast trade and a good few of them also utilise one of their flatter fields for basic camping facilities. It is work that fits in well with life on the farm, and can also give some visitors that extra little insight that makes the holiday special; and of course it has become a crucial part of the farm income. It is not just "B&B" and camping however; a few farms set aside part of their buildings as small cafes, and the valley also has a trout farm supplying to local hotels and restaurants. Such diversification proves to be prudent in the modern day economy of the Lake District.

INTO THE HIGH FELLS

Beyond Rosthwaite the main valley forms a graceful curve around the ancient oaks of Johnny Wood and passes once more into a seemingly new area where the influence and presence of the fells becomes more keenly felt. The terraced cottages of the aptly named Mountain View provide a reminder that, in days gone by, Honister Quarries, at the top of the pass, were a major employer within the area. The same applies at the small, but lovely hamlet of Seatoller. Here there are two terraces of old quarrymens cottages, only a couple of which are permanent residences, the rest having all gone as secondary homes, or as the locals call them, "holiday homes". Now if ever there was a controversial topic in rural societies then this is it, and certainly in Borrowdale there are few people without a thought on the subject. At Seatoller the main valley road starts its long climb over Honister Pass, making a tenuous link with the adjoining valley of Buttermere, providing an important line of social communication between the two dales, and also a crucial and exciting

Setting out

Opposite: The awesome riven flanks of the Scafell range

75

part of the celebrated "Buttermere Round" tourist excursion. It is also from Seatoller that the final stage of Borrowdale, the Seathwaite valley is entered. The valley bottom is still amazingly flat, but now on either side the hillsides rear up steeply and ahead are exciting views of the big fells that dominate the head of the valley.

After a mile the farm buildings of Seathwaite are reached. Seathwaite.... just a farm, a cafe, a cottage and a few barns, and yet the name is renowned throughout the hill walking fraternity of Britain as one of the classic starting points for excursions into the hills. If only the farmer here had a pound for every pair of feet that have traversed his neatly cobbled farm yard! It certainly is an inspirational place, nestling in the valley at the foot of the foaming cascades of Sour Milk Gill, while beyond the strath opens up drawing the eyes enticingly towards the big fells. On a bright summers morning, with the prospect of a good day ahead, there are few finer places.

On a fine day that is, for often it seems that fine days are few and far between at this particular location; indeed at times it seems that there should be a new colour added to the artists pallet.....Seathwaite Grey. If the Edmondsons who farm here are not actually born in waterproofs, they certainly spend a lot of their waking hours in them! This may be a little unfair to Seathwaite, for it is almost certain that farms such as Burnthwaite at Wasdale and Brotherilkeld at Eskdale, in fact any farm at the head of the valleys that penetrate deep into this central massif will receive rather more than its fair share of rain. It is just that the record books name Seathwaite, and it certainly has seen some water. The last big flood here was in 1966 when the valley became a swirling mass of water and the area was declared a disaster zone. Tales of that night, the car that finished up perched on a wall, the Rosthwaite settee that turned up in a living room in Grange, are becoming the stuff of legends.

Seathwaite: The last inhabitance

Long before fellwalking became popular, and even before rainfall figures were recorded, Seathwaite was famous for producing a commodity uniquely (in this country) its own.... Black-Cawke, Plumbago, Graphite, Wadd, call it what you will, this is the raw material that the world famous Cumberland Pencil industry was built on. The old spoil tips to the north of Sour Milk Gill indicate the various stages of the workings which were extensive enough to stretch from the bottom of the fell right up to the plateau some 1,000ft above. Being almost pure carbon the nature of the wadd is vegetable rather than mineral, and evidently was found in the form of tubes or "pipes" which, when excavated formed long shafts. It should be unnecessary to state therefore that internal exploration of these workings is potentially dangerous and should not be undertaken.

Legend has it that a local farmer first discovered the wadd underneath an ash tree uprooted during a storm, and that the shepherds used it to mark their sheep. It was not long however before commercial uses were found, and by the end of the 16th century the lode was being worked on a regular basis. Production slowly increased to reach its heyday in the 18th and early 19th century. Once a pipe was discovered the material was relatively easy to work and therefore, in order to maintain

The Plumbago Mines and Rainguage Cottage

the price, the mines were periodically closed while the buyers worked their way through their stockpiles. It was because of these stockpiles that the Keswick pencil mills could still use Borrowdale wadd some forty years after the mines finally closed.

During the mines' main period of production the wadd was not only used for pencil making, but was also used in the manufacture of "bomb-shells, round-shot, and cannon-balls", all very useful considering the number of wars being fought during the period. It also performed minor miracles in the treatment of "the colic". Such was its value during this period that wadd smuggling became rife, and it was common to see the lanterns of many "pickers" moving over the upper tips under cover of darkness. The Dixons who were then stewards of the mine and lived in what is now Rainguage Cottage, kept a blunderbuss however, and one shot from this would "mak them run like clipt hens". The firearm proved very necessary when in 1751 things got a trifle out of hand as a gang, supposedly of local men organised to steal the wadd, attacked the stewards house. This was serious enough for an Act of Parliament to be passed in 1752 making it " felony to break into any mine or wadd hole of wadd ....or to steal from thence...". When Gilberts Level was driven in 1789 things had reached such a state that a security house was built over the entrance and the miners were strip searched as they left the mine. In some respect the smuggling was understandable as a good nights work on the tips could be more rewarding than a weeks labouring at Honister Quarry or on the local farms, ... but there was always Dixons' blunderbuss to reckon with.

Although there had perhaps been a small pencil producing industry in Keswick from early times, nothing was produced on a mass basis until the start of the 19th century. Soon several mills had opened and these used the best quality Borrowdale Wadd along with cedar wood imported from the United States. The superior quality of the pencils soon became apparent and the businesses thrived, one of them, Banks and

Co. exhibited at the Great Exhibition of 1851 at the Crystal Palace, and again in the Exhibition of 1862. It is probably no coincidence that the growth of this industry came at a time when Keswick had been placed firmly on the map by the tourist industry. From around 1850 imports of cheaper foreign graphite invaded the market and it was not long before the Borrowdale mines closed for good. By using their stockpiles the Keswick manufacturers continued to make good quality pencils from Seathwaite wadd until 1906 when they too turned to the cheaper imports. The industry still flourishes today and is now a sub-division of the Rexel group. It is a major employer at Keswick and is one of the few factories to be found within the National Park. And, of course, Cumberland Pencils are still known the world over.

The visitors who come to Seathwaite to see the wadd mines (fascinating as they are) must be few in number. The vast majority of people who come here are relishing a grand day in the hills. Given the right weather, Seathwaite will not disappoint, for here the fells are as grand as anywhere in Britain. The fells at the head of Borrowdale are all part of the great central massif of the Lake District, and are more rugged and wild, and certainly untamed, than in any other part of the Lakes, indeed many of them take on the character of mountains and in winter need to be treated with the same sort of respect as their loftier brethren might demand. The peaks of this great massif form the mountainous heart of the District and all have great strength, great height and a great nobility. Witness the soaring crags of Scafell and Great End; witness the shapely peaks of Bowfell and Gable; and witness most of all, the rugged aloofness of Scafell Pike, for there is no higher, nor rougher land in England than this. There are no pretenders amongst these greater ranks; there is no room for a pretty Silver How; a sleek, streamlined Catbells; not even a mountain in miniature such as Castle Crag can get a footing here. No, these fells reign supreme, and to walk among them is not only to feel nature in the raw, but also to feel the inspiration of the wild places.

Seathwaite, with one obvious exception, is surrounded by high fells, the eastern side of the valley in particular is walled in by the steep, unbreached flanks of Glaramara. Fortunately the cascading gills that form the head-waters of the River Derwent cut deep into the massif, and the paths that lead into the hills initially follow these natural lines of weakness, prior to gaining the high ridges of the rough fells. From the farm the valley continues into the hills for a reasonably flat three quarters of a mile. This is a respite, a prelude, something to get the legs working, because at the beautiful arch of Stockley Bridge flatness ends and steepness begins. Here there is a parting of the ways; the natural continuation of the valley is Grains Gill; the other path, climbing immediately away from the bridge is the ancient packhorse route to Styhead and Wasdale. This is a crucial junction; it is a sad and pitiful sight watching a walker bound for Gable flogging his way up Grains Gill!

Styhead takes its name from the Norse word Stee meaning ladder and, until the 1,000ft boulder is reached, it feels very appropriate, beyond however the contours ease and soon the shores of the delightful Styhead Tarn are gained. Set in a grassy bowl, the tarn is a green oasis in a land of grey, a shimmering delicacy in a magnificently gaunt mountainous landscape. Another short pull then leads to the Mountain Rescue box on the pass itself, and a major junction of paths. Ahead the slopes descend to the green fields of Wasdale; westwards and all too obvious are the steep sterile screes of Great Gable; but the views that rivet the attention are the awesome riven flanks of the Scafell range, and the brooding northern crags of Lingmell towering over the fissured ravine of Piers Gill, a picture of wild delight.

The great central massif has been breached, Styhead representing the only relatively easy crossing in any direction, so it is not surprising that the route has been used since time immemorial, and indeed up to the present century it was regularly maintained. Nowadays it is a springboard for many ascents of the surrounding fells; the steep stony plod – two feet up one foot back – direct to the summit of Gable; the

alternative route from the tarn up Aaron Slack to Windy Gap; and the climbers way via the South traverse and the wonderfully alpine Napes ridges – superlative climbing. Styhead is also the starting point for a direct route up to Great End and from roughly the same point the famous "Corridor" route sets out on its intricate course across the craggy western flank of the Scafell range. It is amazing that any route at all could traverse such challenging terrain, yet alone one so relatively easy as the Corridor. Many people take this path to Scafell Pike but the route is perhaps better in descent, the ascent being saved for an even better way from Seathwaite.

Another major path heads eastwards from Styhead, ascending close to a ravine bearing the infant Derwent. It emerges on a plateau and shortly reaches the curiously fish-shaped Sprinkling Tarn. This is a special place, for here in amongst the hummocks left by the departed glaciers is the traditional birthplace of the Derwent, the finest of all Lakeland rivers. At an altitude of 2,000ft and nestling beneath the towering precipices of Great End, the setting is appropriately grand. Sprinkling Tarn is a relatively modern name for the place. In days gone by it was known as Prentibjorns Tern, the home of Bjorn the Outlaw, nowadays it is, along with Styhead Tarn, the home of Sid the Wilderness Camper. Sprinkling is a nice enough name, but Prentibjorn has both the romance and sense of heritage that matches the setting. The people who re-named it Sprinkling had no soul!

Continuing beyond the tarn the path crosses the lower of the two Esk Hauses before dropping down to the darkly forbidding Angle Tarn lying in its deep ice carved bowl beneath the frowning crags of Bowfell. It is a very stern birthplace for the river that waters such a beautiful valley as Stonethwaite. The path then climbs once more to Rosset Pass before plummeting down to Mickleden and Langdale. Once more the roots of this path lie shrouded in history but certainly by medieval times it formed a critical part of the network of packhorse routes that criss-crossed the rough fells.

There are other routes from Seathwaite and two of these start from under the arch opposite the farmhouse. This start is all too often missed, a source of embarrassment when the farmer is watching, but once found it is difficult to go wrong. After crossing the river the path once again divides, one path climbing steeply by the side of Sour Milk Gill (awesome when the beck is in spate), the other providing an alternative route to Styhead. This latter path, although initially marshy and indistinct, develops into a mildly adventurous scramble, and, just by the most interestingly positioned gate, gives a stunning view of Taylor Gill Force, the Derwent's only major waterfall. Here Styhead Gill pours over a rockface, crashing 60ft onto the rocks below, providing the most dramatic scene in the entire course of the river. Quite why the waters of Styhead Gill should suddenly become Taylor Gill is a mystery that has never been satisfactorily explained.

The source of the Derwent: Sprinkling Tarn

Back at the farm the Sour Milk Gill path leads upwards, excruciatingly ever upwards, into the remarkable hanging valley of Gillercombe. From the brink of the highest cascade there is a remarkable aerial view of Seathwaite, now looking tiny and remote... another world. Then the great cwm is entered and once more there is silence, but it is doubtful whether solitude will be experienced, this being one of the most popular approaches to Gable. The cwm is overlooked by the 350ft bastion of Raven Crag, known more familiarly to climbers as Gillercombe Buttress, which is seen to good effect from the main path which keeps a safe distance on the other side of the corrie before climbing steeply on its way to Green Gable, the appropriately named Windy Gap, and thence to Great Gable.

In amongst the big fells

There is one final mountain path to be considered, this being the one that follows the valley of Grains Gill away from Stockley Bridge. This is a long grind but the valley has several levels and there are flatter sections to ease the way, and, if the steeper parts should prove too much, there are stunning views of waterfalls and ravines to act as a distraction. Almost throughout, the path is dominated by the towering cliffs of Great End. In certain conditions they almost seem to be frowning down, glowering at the puny person invading the great sanctuary of the massif.

The gradients ease as the aptly named Ruddy Gill is crossed and the main Esk Hause path is joined. Sprinkling Tarn is easily reached from here and a splendid circular walk can be made by descending to Styhead and from there back to Seathwaite. This however is not the main purpose of the steep haul up Grains Gill, nor has it ever been. Historically the Gill was used as a direct route over the upper Esk Hause to Eskdale, and it also acted as a short cut to the main path to Langdale, thereby avoiding the dog leg of the Styhead route. Nowadays the track has been adopted by fellwalkers and forms the royal route to Scafell Pike.

After Ruddy Gill the path climbs steadily to the true (upper) Esk Hause and it is during this section that the true quality of the ascent is felt. Up to now the rift of Grains Gill, deeply enfolded in the hills, has provided a sheltered, comforting approach, but as the pass is approached there is a dawning realisation of being high, very high indeed, and from the Hause onwards the feeling is of being out on the tops. This is what makes Grains Gill so special, for there is nowhere else in Lakeland where there is such a magical transition from the sanctuary of the valley to the exposure of the fell top.

From Esk Hause the well trodden path climbs steadily to the col at the top of Calf Cove and from there it is a literal hop, skip, and jump, with spirits soaring and glory all around, over the bouldery summits of Ill Crag and Broad Crag, before the final stiff pull and ultimate fulfilment at the summit of the highest peak in England. Combined with a descent of the Corridor Route to Styhead (with Gable in magnificent view every step of the way) this is possibly the best mountain day the Lake District has to offer.

Scafell Pike is a magnificent outing and by the time the col at the top of Calf Cove is gained, very few people turn aside to make the detour to the top of Great End, but for Borrowdale this is the Greatest End of all. Here, at the top of the great crags that earlier seemed so daunting, all is laid out before. Almost a thousand feet below lies Sprinkling Tarn; is it the beginning, or is it an end? Or is it neither; for surely here is something that will last for eternity? As Wordsworth put it:

> "..as I cast my eyes,
> I see what was, and is, and will abide;
> Still glides the Stream, and shall for ever glide;
> The Form remains, the Function never dies;"

But will it be the same Borrowdale in the future? Will this beautiful valley inspire the thousands to come, as it has the thousands before? And if it does will the land be able to cope? It is a strong land, a land of mountains that are not easily destroyed, but it is also a fragile land, easily despoiled, sometimes even at the hands of those who love it most. It is a valley that has given something to a lot of people and asks nothing in return. Those who have been blessed by its riches will return time and time again, and each time it will be viewed afresh. A land as special as this needs to be cherished; the land, and the people who have done so much to nurture this beauty, deserve to be respected. Here, on the edge of all things, look out and be glad for what Borrowdale has given you.